Praise for
When the Word Leads Your Pastoral Search

The next time someone asks me for advice on conducting a pastoral search process I will tell him to read this book. This isn't the only book you should read prior to launching your search, but it is the first. This book is practical, theological, biblical, and wise. And when a pertinent topic isn't covered, Chris Brauns points you to the right resources. There are few decisions more crucial for a church than picking the right pastor. You owe it to yourself to read this book. It will help churches and pastors avoid lots of common mistakes.

—Kevin DeYoung, Senior Pastor,
University Reformed Church (East Lansing, MI)

In the normal course of events, the search for a pastor should not be a regular event in the life of a congregation. When a church needs to find a pastor, therefore, many have little guidance as to how to go about the process. Chris Brauns's book is the only resource of its kind that I have ever seen. If your church is searching for a pastor, or if you are a pastor seeking to equip your congregation to follow biblical guidelines when that day does come, I highly recommend this thoughtful, practical, biblical work to you.

—Russell D. Moore, Dean,
The Southern Baptist Theological Seminary

A high percentage of pastoral searches are triggered by conflict, which is a frequent reason churches lose one pastor and start looking for another. If the next fit is not good, the cycle will only repeat itself. This is why I am eager to recommend Chris's book to every church that is looking for a new pastor. By drawing on the wisdom of God's Word, Chris will help you get it right
some fun in the process.

—Ken Sande, Presid
Peacemaker Minis

You will have no higher responsibility that the one entrusted to you now. You are asked to help choose the next pastor for your congregation. The person you choose will be charged with teaching God's Word to the assembled church Sunday after Sunday. It is not the only task assigned to a pastor but it is an essential task. It resembles passing for a quarterback in football. He must do more than throw the football; but if he can't pass he cannot play the position.

You will be wise as a committee to seek for guidance in your selection. I heartily recommend *When the Word Leads Your Pastoral Search* by Chris Brauns as a tool to guide you to an effective biblical preacher to teach and lead your church. Read it; study it; and act on it. You will be helped and your church will benefit.

—Haddon Robinson
Harold John Ockenga Professor of Preaching
Gordon-Conwell Theological Seminary

When a church is looking for a pastor, its first priority must be to find a preacher. Preaching is not all a pastor is called to do, but it is the central, nonnegotiable task of ministry. Thus, a clear understanding of the preaching task is the responsibility of those conducting the search for a new pastor so that they will faithfully fulfill their charge. This book provides sound, biblically based advice and counsel that congregations and search committees will find to be invaluable, as will pastors who will come to a clearer understanding of their own calling.

—Dr. R. Albert Mohler, President,
The Southern Baptist Theological Seminary

The pastoral search process can be confusing and intimidating, especially in the hands of lay people who have never faced such a weighty responsibility before. Too many search committees let pragmatic concerns rather than biblical principles determine their course of action, and that is a recipe for disaster. Chris Brauns shows us a better way. Pastoral search committees will find this book an immensely helpful resource.

—John MacArthur, Pastor and Teacher
Grace Community Church

When the Word Leads Your Pastoral Search

Biblical Principles & Practices to Guide Your Search

Chris Brauns

Moody Publishers
Chicago

Edited by Jim Vincent
Interior design: Ragont Design
Cover design: John Hamilton Design, LLC
Cover image: iStock

Library of Congress Cataloging-in-Publication Data

Brauns, Chris
When the word leads your pastoral search : Biblical principles and practices to guide your search / Chris Brauns.
p. cm.
Includes bibliographical references.
ISBN 978-0-8024-4984-9
1. Clergy—Appointment, call, and election. 2. Pastoral search committees. I. Title.
BV664.B74 2011
254—dc22

2010032503

We hope you enjoy this book from Moody Publishers. Our goal is to provide high-quality, thought-provoking books and products that connect truth to your real needs and challenges. For more information on other books and products written and produced from a biblical perspective, go to www.moodypublishers.com or write to:

Moody Publishers
820 N. LaSalle Boulevard
Chicago, IL 60610

3 5 7 9 10 8 6 4 2

Printed in the United States of America

For the "Bricks in the Valley" who have remembered that
God makes bricks with a building in mind,
and who, like the Bereans,
receive God's Word eagerly

Contents

Acknowledgments

No one writes a book alone. I am thankful for many people who had a part in this one.

Once again, Joy McCarnan not only endured my "uber-weird" drafts, but also made significant improvements. Thanks also to my agent, Tim Beals of Credo Communications.

I grew up hearing stories about D. L. Moody and other nineteenth-century leaders in Chicago, men like Ira Sankey, Phillip Bliss, and Horatio Spafford. As a farm kid in Iowa, I never would have dreamed that I would one day have the opportunity to work with Moody Publishers, and I am hard-pressed to express how honored I am. At Moody, acquisitions editor Dave Dewit and developmental editor Jim Vincent have helped in shaping the manuscript, and Keith Wiederwax, marketing manager, has been a particular encouragement.

Looking back on my time working with my good friend Chip Bernhard, I realize how much I learned from him about being a shepherd who loves the sheep.

I am privileged to serve the "Bricks" at the Congregational Christian Church of Stillman Valley, "The Red Brick Church," where Jana Krause keeps my calendar straight and Terrell Carby has taught me everything he knows about interviewing and human resources, even if he did eat all my wintergreen mints.

Several took time to share their insights as they relate to local churches calling a pastor. Rob Stevenson and Tony Kroening of SIMA International shared from their experience in the field of recruiting. I was privileged to interact with Dr. Albert Mohler and Dr. Russell Moore of Southern Baptist Theological Seminary in Louisville. Tom Boyce, an elder at Elmbrook Church in Brookfield, Wisconsin, also provided valuable insights.

The faculty at both Grand Rapids Theological Seminary and Gordon-Conwell Theological Seminary shaped my thinking in foundational ways and equipped me to think and write about pastoral ministry and the local church. Dr. Haddon Robinson and Dr. Sid Buzzell were great resources when I first wrote about this subject for my doctoral thesis at Gordon-Conwell. The annual Gordon-Conwell doctoral retreat at Lake Geneva continues to be one of the greatest encouragements in my life and ministry.

My children, Allison, Chris, Ben, and Mary Beth, remind me when it's 10:40 even while they have endured another writing project on my behalf. I am more thankful for their love and support than they can know.

My pretty, smiling wife, Jamie, continues to be the greatest gift that God has given me. I cannot imagine a more supportive or encouraging wife.

Ultimately, all praise and glory must go to the Lord Jesus Christ, who is the Good Shepherd (John 10), the Great Shepherd (Hebrews 13:20–21), and the Chief Shepherd (1 Peter 5:4).

ANYONE WHO HAS WATCHED a relay race knows that the race is often won or lost by how well the baton is passed.

Carolyn Weese
The Elephant in the Boardroom

COMMIT YOUR WORK to the Lord, and your plans will be established.

Proverbs 16:3

AND WE HAVE SOMETHING more sure, the prophetic word, to which you will do well to pay attention as to a lamp shining in a dark place, until the day dawns and the morning star rises in your hearts.

2 Peter 1:19

Introduction

I was never any good at dating. So if I were part of a church preparing to call a pastor, and if I were to read a book comparing the pastoral call to courtship, it would immediately provoke some awkward memories.

Still, it ought to be said: A pastoral search parallels dating at every stage of the relationship. In the beginning, potential candidates get a phone call from some mutual acquaintance. The mutual acquaintance makes small talk and then nonchalantly asks, "Do you know that nice-looking church over by Des Moines? She thinks you're cute. Are you interested in her?"

It goes from there. Both parties dispatch e-mails.

Everyone Googles. The really committed ones may even tweet or text. (And if you don't know what "tweeting" is, don't worry about it. You're probably better off.)

The parallel continues throughout the relationship. Eventually, a church decides it's time to "propose," at which point "premarital" counseling questions are in order. As a pastor, I always ask engaged couples, "Why do you think your home will succeed when so many fail?"

Similarly, we might ask a church calling a pastor, "Why do you think calling this pastor will be successful, when so many pastorates end in the ditch? Indeed, it may be that the reason your church is looking for a pastor is because the previous pastor left amid tension and disagreement. Surely, you were well-intentioned when you called that pastor. Why will this time be any different?"

It doesn't work to mutter, "It will be different because we are calling a different pastor." That is as naïve as a pastor assuming that the next church will be different than the one he is leaving where he just had a bad experience.

In premarital counseling, once I have done my best to shake up young couples who haven't really thought about why they can be confident in their future, I share with them the only proper basis for being optimistic about their new home. Psalm 127:1 reads, "Unless the Lord builds the house, those who build it labor in vain. Unless the Lord watches over the city, the watchman stays awake in vain." If God builds our homes, we can look forward to a future He will bless. "What we want to do in premarital counseling," I tell them, "is understand very specifically what it will look like for the Lord to build your house."

My aim here is the same. I want to show you that the only way your search for a pastor can succeed is if it is shaped by an understanding of Scriptures. God's Word is what gives light to the eyes and makes wise the simple (Psalm 19:7–10). We must look to it as to a light shining in a dark place (2 Peter 1:19–21). Together, let's consider what the Bible says about what a pastor should be and do so that your church can be sure that God is building your house when you call your next pastor.

Don't get me wrong. I don't mean to imply that a commitment to Christ and His Word will be something new for your church. But for any local church, committing to the Word of Christ is never something we do just one time. We do it over and over again, and with each new situation we need to see in both specific and concrete ways how God's Word comes to bear. The situation you now face is that of calling a pastor, and for that task the twofold goal of this book is to motivate you to be Word-centered and to show you practically how to go about it.

As we prepare to look toward biblical ideals in this book, keep in mind that just as your church is not perfect, neither will any candidate be perfect. While you should strive to look for a godly pastor, don't find yourself looking for the next great leader in the Christian world. As D. A. Carson has reminded pastors like me:

> Most of us, however, serve in more modest patches. Most pastors will not preach to thousands. They will not write influential books, they will not supervise large staffs, and they will never see more than

> modest growth. They will plug away at their care of the aged, at their visitation, at their counseling, at their Bible studies and preaching . . . Most of us—let us be frank—are ordinary pastors.[1]

That is who I am, an ordinary pastor. Chances are you are part of an ordinary church. So don't insist on perfection. Rather, let the Word lead your search and look for a pastor who is not a superstar, but rather is humble and contrite in spirit, and trembles at the Word (Isaiah 66:1–2).

Here are a few other introductory observations. While the explicit focus of this book is on calling a lead or senior pastor, I pray that this book will be a resource to those filling pastoral positions beyond those. The principles used here have direct application for calling any church leader. For instance, if you are calling a youth pastor, then your young people need a pastor who will preach the Word in youth group meetings. A potential youth pastor's preaching or teaching could be evaluated in the same ways I will outline here.

I am also praying that this book will be used to encourage pastors. Perhaps some pastors might use this book to summarize what they believe about the priorities for a pastor, noting, of course, areas where they disagree with my convictions.

This book is not meant to provide a suggested administrative approach with flow diagrams and letters or the details of the process. The administrative operations will differ from church to church, depending on your particular setting. There *are* some very helpful procedural guides available depending on your denomination or fellowship (see recommended reading on page 185).

Nor will this book offer varied counsel specific to churches of various sizes. I recognize that how a church looks for a pastor will differ quite a bit depending on the size of the congregation. Yet this book will outline biblical principles and practices that are applicable whether you are a church of sixty or a church of six thousand.

Those of you who have been married for any length of time know that it would be arrogant and naïve for a couple planning to marry to think that they have enough wisdom in themselves to be confident in their marriage. "Unless the Lord builds the house, those who build it labor in vain."

And the same is true for a church looking for a pastor. In and of ourselves, none of us has the wisdom that will ensure God's blessing on a pastoral search. That wisdom is found only in the Word of God. My prayer is that this book will be used to encourage your church to be absolutely determined to look to the Word as you seek to call your next pastor.

Note

1. D. A. Carson, *Memoirs of an Ordinary Pastor* (Wheaton, Ill.: Crossway, 2008), 9.

Part 1

It's Not What You Know . . .

ANYONE WHO HAS EVER looked very long for a job knows the truth of the old saying, "It's not what you know; it's who you know." Few things are more valuable in finding a job, or filling a position, than an extensive network.

The truth of this saying in mind, the goal of Part 1 is to make sure you know the right group of people. The group I will introduce you to includes:

Moses. In chapter 1 we will reflect on an impossible situation the great leader and Israel faced to learn truths about facing challenges.

The Bereans. chapters 2 and 4 will introduce you to the Bereans, an early group of Christians described in the book of Acts 17:10–15. While we have only six verses about the Bereans, they are a group to add to your network.

A fictional pastoral search committee from First Church. In chapter 3, you will meet a fictional pastoral search committee that doesn't really exist. But they have much in common with the approach of most real pastoral search committees. If this search committee is part of your network, then you may be able to avoid making their mistakes.

A fictional pastoral search committee from Calvary Church. This PSC makes mistakes too; instead we can learn several good pastoral qualities by looking once more at the Bereans.

IF I WISHED TO HUMBLE ANYONE, I should question him about his prayers. I know nothing to compare with this topic for its sorrowful self-confessions.

Dean C. J. Vaughn
As quoted in *Spiritual Leadership* by J. Oswald Sanders

IN THESE DAYS HE WENT OUT to the mountain to pray, and all night he continued in prayer to God. And when day came, he called his disciples and chose from them twelve, whom he named apostles.

Luke 6:12–13a.

1

With Your Back to the Red Sea

Of the two situations that follow, which do you think would be the more difficult prospect for leaders in these two situations? Although you know how one of the two ended, pretend that you don't. Which presents a tougher challenge?

Situation #1: You are Moses leading Israel, and you face a furious Pharaoh and his mighty army. (If you are sketchy on the details of that account, you can read it in Exodus 14.) Pharaoh is unpredictable and has anger management problems. Many of the soldiers are driven by the fury of vengeance for their recently slain firstborn sons. To top it all off, your only escape route is blocked by a very large body of water—the Red Sea.

Situation #2: You are part of a church looking for a pastor. Perhaps you're an elder or part of the pastoral search committee. Or, maybe you are a member of the church. You need to find God's man for your church. This requires identifying a candidate, getting the pastoral search committee to agree, and garnering your church's overwhelming support of the decision. It probably will also require your candidate to leave a church and community where he has built deep ties with people he loves.

So, which is tougher? What do you think?

The goal in this chapter is to persuade you that the search for a new pastor truly is more difficult. A church looking for a pastor faces a more difficult task than Moses and the Israelites faced—at least in one crucial regard.

Of course, you could argue it the other way. After all, with the Egyptians there was potential for fatal violence. Hopefully you won't face that threat with your pastoral search. Certainly, my point is not to minimize God's character and work as evidenced by the Red Sea miracle. As a general principle in antiquity, a large multitude backed up by a powerful army against a body of water didn't have a great future. It is no small thing that God protected and provided for His people in this way.

The Committed Committee

Yet even as we recognize the difficulty of Moses' situation, if we think about it, we'd probably agree that, humanly speaking, the job of calling the right pastor is impossible. To begin with, leaders in your local church face a major time commitment when they say yes to being on a search committee. Many pastoral search committees meet on a weekly basis. Even those search committees that meet less frequently will find their time constrained as they continue with everyday tasks—getting kids to soccer practice, doing household chores, mowing the lawn, and whatever other obligations they already have. For committee members to be able to surrender the necessary hours amid so many demands in life, their hearts will need supernatural softening and strengthening.

Once you've dealt with the scheduling hurdle, your pastoral search committee and/or elders will need to agree about which resources to consult, from where to recruit, what the search priorities are, and most obviously, which candidate to pursue. Coming to an agreement on these sorts of things isn't always easy—even for a small group. Finally your search brings the committee to a pastoral candidate, which will necessitate that dozens or hundreds or, depending on the size of your church, even thousands agree that this candidate is the right choice—even though we know that getting a church to come to a consensus is like herding cats.

The Committed Candidate

The pastoral search process is also difficult because it requires a major commitment and faith by the pastor candidate and his family. Most likely, you will be asking your next pastor and his family to leave a place where their hearts are knit together with people. I think about what that would be like for my family right now to go to a different church. We love our church and community. Three of our four children are teenagers, and humanly speaking, it seems impossible to think of moving them at this point in time. If God were to call us away, it would feel like being torn in half.

You might respond, "While it's true that a church looking for a pastor has a difficult job, it still seems to me that Moses had it worse. The laws of physics being what they are, there seemed to be absolutely no escape for Moses. There was every reason the people should be slaughtered without mercy on the beach and that whoever might survive would be driven right back to Egypt and right back into slavery."

Do It Yourself

Yet I think the clear impossibility of the Red Sea situation is why it was easier on one level. In the case of the Red Sea, the realists in the crowd—just about everyone—would have quickly recognized that there was nothing they could accomplish to get out of the mess. Their only hope was to throw themselves at the feet of God and pray that He would deliver them. Exodus 14:10 says that the Israelites cried out to the Lord (in addition to blaming Moses [v. 11]).

Contrast this with a pastoral search. Whether or not it is true in your church, the reality is that most pastoral search committees struggle with a presupposition of self-sufficiency. While they would never admit to themselves or one another that they think they can figure out a pastor on their own, this is the assumption they live out. Many pastoral search committees believe they need no help from beyond their local church. Apart from being willing to heed the input of district leaders or other wise people, most searchers honestly believe they can (and that they must) handle the search completely on their own.

The biggest clue to the self-reliance felt by pastoral search committees is the small amount of attention they devote to prayer. Prayer is the "dental floss" of pastoral searches: something we know we should use but, more often than not, leave at home.

Why is it that churches looking for pastors *know* that they *need* to pray, yet *don't* pray? As I have said, the answer is a false sense of self-sufficiency. Churches think they can do this thing—this *impossible* thing—in their own strength. It was the distinct advantage of the Israelites when they were fleeing from the Egyptians that they *knew* that they were in trouble and that they couldn't possibly get out of the mess they were in on their own. So they cried out to God. And this is where we need to be. Any time we truly realize that we face an impossible situation, it will do wonders for our prayer lives. That is where you need to be as a pastoral search committee.

Behind the Scenes: Prayer

The necessity of prayer during recruitment is seen in the example of our King. These verses from Luke are extremely relevant for a church looking for a pastor:

In these days [Jesus] went out to the mountain to pray, and all night he continued in prayer to God. And when day came, he called his disciples and chose from them twelve, whom he named apostles: Simon, whom he named Peter, and Andrew his brother, and James and John, and Philip, and Bartholomew, and Matthew, and Thomas, and James the son of Alphaeus, and Simon who was called the Zealot. (Luke 6:12–15)

Here was Jesus, chairman of the only *perfect* search committee of one. He had *perfect* wisdom and discernment. He was the greatest recruiter in the history of humanity. Yet before He met with candidates for spots on His team, He spent the night in prayer.

Similarly, prayer is necessary for each search committee member as he and she seek to find the right pastor. That's how they did it in the early church, as they sought elders to lead and pastor the sheep:

And after they had preached the gospel to that city and had made many disciples, they returned to Lystra and to Iconium and to Antioch, strengthening the souls of the disciples, encouraging them to continue in the faith, and saying, "Through many tribulations we must enter the kingdom of God." When they had appointed elders for them in every church, having prayed with fasting, *they commended them to the Lord in whom they had believed. They passed through Pisidia and came into Pamphylia. When they had spoken the word in Perga, they went down to Attalia.* (Acts 14:21–25 NASB; emphasis added)

Notice that the text says that with prayer and fasting they appointed elders for them in each church. Prayer continued throughout the entire process, and the early church rightly associated prayer and fasting with calling pastors.

Prayer is essential at every stage of your pastoral search, from choosing a pastoral search committee to praying for your next pastor. Be sure you do more than just talk about praying. What your local church really needs to do is organize prayer and actually put it into practice. At the end of the pastoral search process, you are going to want assurance that you sought and received God's provision, not your own solutions. That assurance will come in part from knowing that God answered your prayers for those things! It's not a matter of whether you agree that prayer is important. It's a given that prayer *is* essential. Therefore your assurance of a right choice is going to hinge on how that prayer infiltrated the search process. Assurance rises when you can answer positively the following kinds of questions:

- Did the elders put anyone specifically in charge of organizing prayer during your pastoral search?
- When the pastoral search team met, did they spend more time actually praying . . . or making small talk and discussing candidates to pray over?
- Did the elders and those filling the pulpit for the interim teach the congregation about the central importance of prayer through a study of biblical prayers?
- Did the elders encourage your congregation to fast (giving up either food or something else)? Recall

that Jesus said, "Whenever you fast" (Matthew 6:16)—the assumption being that His people would sometimes fast.

- Did you have organized times of congregational prayer when a great number of your people participated? A great idea is to designate a "prayer room" for use before church on Sunday mornings. Your people will already be at church for morning services, and it will not require another night set aside in the week. Did you as a church publish specific prayer requests for the pastoral search?
- Did you encourage your church family to keep prayer journals in which to write out their own prayers for the pastoral search process?
- Did your elders, deacons, and pastoral search committee keep one another accountable for how much and how seriously you prayed for the pastoral search?

Specific Prayer Suggestions

In response to the challenge questions above, you might ask, "How exactly should we pray during our pastoral search?" The following are specific prayer suggestions. They don't comprise an exhaustive list, but are a good place to begin. I have divided this list into three parts. The first part suggests ways you can pray for your search committee. The second part describes specific ways to pray for your next pastor. And the third part outlines ways to pray for the congregation.

1. Pray for the Search Committee

Here are four areas to pray for on behalf of your search:

- *Pray for patience.* Pray that the group would wait for God's timing.
- *Pray that your search committee will have the mind of Christ and agree.* Much of the process is subjective. Personal opinions and preferences are involved. Differences can divide. Ask that they would heed Paul's advice for unity, having the humble attitude of Jesus Christ (Philippians 2:1–12, especially verse 5). It is so easy for us consciously—or more often, unconsciously—to bring our own agendas into church business.
- *Pray for wisdom to choose the right person.* Pray that the pastoral search committee will renew their minds in the Bible so that they can have Word-centered wisdom (Romans 12:1–2).
- *Pray for discipline for your search committee and other church leaders.* The search process will require a great deal of follow-through on the parts of individuals. It will also require that they not digress from the agenda or retrace decisions they have already made. Pray for unity and agreement between your elders and the pastoral search committee.

2. Pray for Your Next Pastor

Here are five ways you can pray for the future pastor during the search process:

- *Pray that God would increase his passion for preaching the Word of God.*
- *Pray that God would give him a love for your church and the strength to leave his current position* (if the candidate senses that is God's direction).
- *Pray that your next pastor would begin new relationships at your church in the right way*, even during the search process.
- *Pray that God would prepare your future pastor to shepherd your flock more effectively* through the trials and blessings he has faced or currently faces.
- *Pray for your next pastor's family.* Of course, he may be single or married. He may have children or not. God knows all that. Pray that God, who knows each detail about each member of your pastor's household, would give the members of his family strength as they consider leaving their current setting and going to a different church, or beginning pastoral ministry for the first time.

3. Pray for the People in Your Church

Here are three ways you can pray on behalf of your church family during the upcoming search:

- *Pray for patience.* The search process can go on longer than expected. It is hard for people doing the work of searching. It is also difficult for those in the congregation who must wait without knowing exactly what is going on. Pray that your people would trust the leadership and uphold you during the whole process.

- *Pray that your people would learn to place a high priority on biblical preaching.* It is easy to gravitate toward personality, programs, a particular "ideal" age, etc. Pray that, above all, the congregation would call a pastor who will proclaim the Word without apology.
- *Pray that your people would not react to a previous pastor.* Some churches struggle with wanting a pastor who is like their old one (they had a good experience). Other churches want someone who is just the opposite. (See "Mistake to avoid #9," page 176.)

The Summary Word

Imagine how earnestly you or I would pray if we found ourselves pinned by Pharaoh's massive army against the Red Sea. It is this same sort of urgency in prayer that we need to bring to the search for a pastor. If your church can remember the impossibility of succeeding on their own, then you will be a people of prayer during your search for a pastor.

One of your first priorities in prayer should be to pray for the formation of your pastoral search committee. The next chapter will introduce you to a group of people who will help you know how to pray about that important step in your search for a pastor.

LUKE OBVIOUSLY ADMIRES [the Bereans'] enthusiasm for Paul's preaching, together with their industry and unprejudiced openness in studying the Scriptures. They combined receptivity with critical questioning.

John Stott
The Spirit, the Word, the Church

NOW THESE JEWS WERE MORE NOBLE than those in Thessalonica; they received the word with all eagerness, examining the Scriptures daily to see if these things were so.

Acts 17:11

2

Lessons from the Bereans

So, how's it going with naming the pastoral search committee?" Jennie Creston asked her husband, Lon, an elder at the church. Because Lon didn't arrive home from last night's elder meeting to nominate search committee members until after midnight, she wondered if the meeting hadn't gone well.

Jennie wasn't really expecting a happy answer, but she was surprised at the intensity and frustration in Lon's response. He slammed shut a cabinet door and began to vent. "It's a mess—just a total mess! People who *should* be on the search committee have already told us they won't accept a position. They're mostly too busy, but Dick told me today that his main reason for bowing out is that he doesn't want to get caught in the middle of a churchwide fight.

"On top of that, the elders got these three e-mails from different church members expressing their own opinions about who the elders ought to nominate for the search committee. Some elders think we should just nominate one committee member from every ministry in the church, including one of the teens from the youth group. So far, I think the only thing the elders *do* agree on is that we all have a headache! How do *you* think we should select the pastoral search committee?"

Finding the Right Members

At some point early in your search for a new pastor, your church must identify the group who will take leadership in evaluating potential candidates. In some churches, this group will be called the "pastoral nominating committee." In others, the elders themselves will evaluate pastoral candidates. Still other churches will call this group the "pastoral search committee"—which is the label I will use here.

However your pastoral search committee is selected, it is critical that it be composed of the right people. Indeed, if there is one common thread in the materials that I have read, it's that the careful forming of the right pastoral search committee is probably the single most important factor in the successful calling of the right pastor. Yet, churches like Lon and Jennie's fictional one struggle to know what to look for in pastoral search committee members.

Unless your church uses its elders to do double duty, your church will need to select the right members for the nominating or search committee. What *should* a church be looking for in pastoral search committee members? Or, if you have already selected a pastoral search committee, what qualities should you seek to develop as a pastoral search committee? In this chapter and the next two we will look at the biblical example of the Bereans (Acts 17:10–15) for the answers to these questions.

Two Key Qualities of the Bereans

While we don't know a lot about the people in Berea, we know two things that are of great interest to churches looking for a pastor. First, Scripture declares that they were "more noble" (Acts 17:11). The comparison here is to Thessalonica, where a riot broke out when the Word was preached. In contrast to this chaos, God's Word affirms the Bereans. What church wouldn't aspire to be commended in this way by the Bible?

Acts also records that the Bereans influenced others. Reading of what happened in Berea when the Word was preached, we see, "Many of them therefore believed, with not a few Greek women of high standing as well as men" (v.12). When we recall the ongoing tensions that existed between Jews and Gentiles at the beginning of the church, it is striking to consider that while Paul began with the Jews in the synagogues, the gospel immediately spread to community leaders amongst the Greeks. Effective leadership took place in Berea.

This combination of pleasing God and leading the

community is a good summary of what a church looking for a pastor is trying to accomplish. If at the end of the pastoral search, the chairman of your leadership team could announce, "We believe that God is pleased and our congregation supports the decision," then you will be assured your search for a pastor was blessed.

The passage on the Berean believers is very instructive. You may want to read these verses aloud:

> *The brothers immediately sent Paul and Silas away by night to Berea, and when they arrived they went into the Jewish synagogue. Now these Jews were more noble than those in Thessalonica; they received the word with all eagerness, examining the Scriptures daily to see if these things were so. Many of them therefore believed, with not a few Greek women of high standing as well as men. But when the Jews from Thessalonica learned that the word of God was proclaimed by Paul at Berea also, they came there too, agitating and stirring up the crowds. Then the brothers immediately sent Paul off on his way to the sea, but Silas and Timothy remained there. Those who conducted Paul brought him as far as Athens, and after receiving a command for Silas and Timothy to come to him as soon as possible, they departed.* (Acts 17:10–15)

The Word-Centered Bereans

The core cause of the commendation for the Bereans is their focus on the Word: "They received the word with all eagerness, examining the Scriptures" (v. 11). This emphasis on the Word is no incidental detail. One of the continuing emphases of Acts, and the Bible as a whole, is that the gospel goes forth in conjunction with the proclaimed Word (cf. Acts 6:7, 12:24, 19:20).

This priority on being Word-centered is one that must be pursued for churches looking for a pastor. In calling a pastor, your church's first and foremost responsibility is to form a Word-centered pastoral search committee. Of course, there is no separating the written Word of God from our Lord Jesus Christ, who is the Word (John 1:1–5). So when we say, "We're looking for Word-centered pastoral search committee members," we mean not simply that they say they believe the Bible, but that the *defining truth of their lives* is that they profess the Living Word as their Lord and are devoted to the written Word.

Keep in mind that being Word-centered is the foundation of making good decisions. The question, "Which pastor do we call?" falls in the broad area of how believers determine God's direction or will in a particular matter. Basically, the way that Christians make decisions today is through wisdom. Wisdom is "skill for right living." Wisdom is developed through having your mind renewed in the pages of Scripture. Consider Romans 12:2: "Do not be conformed to this world, but be transformed by the renewal of your mind, that by testing you may discern what is the will of God, what is good and acceptable and perfect."

Paul tells his audience that as their minds are renewed, that is as they grow in wisdom, then they will be able to make God's choices regarding God's direction. Paul uses similar thinking in Philippians 1:9–11.

> *And this is my prayer: that your love may abound more and more in knowledge and depth of insight, so that you may be able to discern what is best and may be pure and blameless until the day of Christ, filled with the fruit of righteousness that comes through Jesus Christ—to the glory and praise of God.* (Philippians 1:9–11 NIV)

Paul's prayer for the Philippians is that their love would abound in knowledge and depth of insight in order that they would be able to make discerning choices. In this context, we could easily substitute for "knowledge and depth of insight" the word "wisdom."

You might counter, "Well, we are familiar with those passages. But other passages in Scripture teach other methods. Gideon put out a fleece (Judges 6:36 ff). The early church cast lots (Acts 1:26)." However, not everything that is in the Bible is prescriptive. Some passages are descriptive. In other words, historical accounts in the Bible are often given for a purpose other than setting an example for how we should do things today.

If we took everything as prescriptive, then based on Exodus 3 your search committee might choose to use a "burning bush approach." You could pray that while your next pastor is out working in his yard, one of his bushes would catch on fire without being consumed. While it is possible that God could call your next pastor in that manner, it is not normally how God works today. If you choose that approach, you could be in the desert a long time. After all, most towns don't even allow us to burn leaves!

So, if the point is that the foundational way Christians make decisions is by growing in wisdom through the Word, then you see the importance of having a pastoral search committee that, like the Bereans, is Word-centered.

Two Practical Results of Forming a Word-Centered Pastoral Search Committee

It might help you better see the point if I show you two practical results of forming a Word-centered pastoral search committee.

First, a Word-centered pastoral search committee will evaluate candidates against biblical qualifications. For these groups, the qualifications outlined in 1 Timothy 3:1–7 and Titus 1:6–9 will be a constant.

Beware of including people on your pastoral search committee who are dismissive when biblical requirements for leadership are mentioned in their presence. Often, such a person will say something like, "Well, I'm not the best one to ask what the Bible says. I'll leave it to the rest of the committee to examine him on Bible topics. But I've been around this church for a long time, and I want to make sure—" From there, he or she will go on to stress some pet priority.

In terms of practicality, it is vital that the decision-makers involved are spending time faithfully in the Word of God. You must be renewing your minds continually with the truth of God's Word so that you are equipped and able to make good decisions. A great place for pastoral search committees to begin as a reference point is the Pastoral Epistles, which consist of First and Second Timothy and

Titus. I already mentioned those specific portions known for delineating "pastoral qualifications" (1 Timothy 3:1–7; Titus 1:6–9). But don't stop with those passages. These three epistles (letters) from Paul to his protégées were written to develop pastoral leadership and are ideal fodder for pastoral search committees' meditation during the search. Indeed, I would encourage everyone involved in your pastoral search to read prayerfully through these three books five to ten times during the course of their search.

The second practical outcome of forming a Word-centered pastoral search committee is that the committee will see the need to call a pastor who will preach the Word. As we will see, being a gifted preacher and teacher is central in calling a pastor, and this is what your church needs. You aren't in need of just another man's slant on life. You don't need a lot of opinions or stories. You need a preacher who will provide for the gnawing hunger of your life. That kind of hunger can be met only through a "meal" of Scripture.

The Summary Word

If your church forms a pastoral search committee that is truly Word-centered, like the Bereans were, then you will be well on your way to pleasing God and leading your people. Because their minds are renewed by God's Word, the committee members will be able to wisely lead your church in calling a pastor. They will evaluate candidates against a biblical standard for pastoral qualifications, target candidates who preach the Word, and—eventually—find and call a new pastor who will continue to lead the church to be Word-centered.

Thinking about all of this, you might respond, "Well, I don't disagree with an emphasis on the Word. But we also need *unity*. If we involve a wide diversity of people from the church on our pastoral search committee (even though they may not be equally committed to the preached Word as a key criterion for choosing), then it might at least help us achieve unity." "Besides," you add, "we want to survey *our people* and ask them what they want in their next pastor."

I agree that unity should be pursued by a local church. The question of how to pursue unity is an important one that deserves a chapter all its own. In fact, we will turn to that next.

IT IS UNION WITH GOD that creates the unity of God's people.

Edmund Clowney
The Church

WHEN [PAUL] WAS FACING the most normal of problems (division in the church, worldliness, selfishness, and others) he reached for deeply theological responses. Paul called the Corinthian congregation not to be divided but united . . . He called them to forsake divisions because God is one.

Mark Dever
Twelve Challenges Churches Face

SO IF THERE IS ANY encouragement in Christ, any comfort from love, any participation in the Spirit, any affection and sympathy, complete my joy by being of the same mind, having the same love, being in full accord and of one mind.

Philippians 2:1–2

3

Unity Requires a Center

"No, no, Mrs. Wiley, I'm not disagreeing with you," said Al Borman, chairman of the First Church pastoral search committee. "I agree. It is important that, according to the survey, 24 percent of our people want the next pastor to make our seniors group more of a priority. But I was hoping that you noticed that in the same survey 22 percent said we should have a pastor who relates well to the young people. We are hearing a couple of different things from our congregation."

Mrs. Wiley was not persuaded. "Don't you see? A full 2 percent more believe older people should be the first priority. Of course, we all love the young people. But *clearly* it will unify our church more to place emphasis on getting a pastor who will relate to the seniors group, which means, as *everyone* knows, we ought to call a pastor who is at least forty-five or even older!"

Mrs. Wiley paused briefly to take a breath. "And *don't forget* that according to the survey, pretty much everyone agrees that our next pastor simply must be more outgoing than Pastor Collins."

Mrs. Wiley paused at this point to see if she had persuaded the search committee chair. When he remained silent, she continued, with a tone of heightened frustration. "What I want to know is, if the elders didn't plan to listen to the majority opinion, why did you even bother to survey the congregation in the first place?"

When Seeking Unity Leads to Disunity

Whatever your system of church government—whether you are congregational or elder-led—you ought to desire unity. Like Paul, we know that there is more joy when God's people are "of the same mind, having the same love, being in full accord and of one mind" (Philippians 2:1–2). "It is an honor for a man to keep aloof from strife, but every fool will be quarreling" (Proverbs 20:3).

So we pursue unity. But one of the points I will make in this chapter is that sometimes the very ways that churches try to build unity end up sparking disunity. It's ironic. There are churches that take well-intentioned and carefully measured steps in hopes of seeing their congregations draw closer together, but the result is only increased friction and conflict.

Let me give you two examples of unity strategies that can lead to disunity. First, churches looking for a pastor are often advised to form a pastoral search committee with automatic representation from the most important subgroups in the congregation. Many do. While it is valid and can be helpful to consider input from the representatives of different church ministries, the first requirement for committee member nominees should be that they are Word-centered. As I said in the previous chapter, a Word-centered pastoral search committee will understand the need to call a pastor who will preach the Word. A Word-centered pastoral search committee will also evaluate candidates against biblical qualifications.

But if different groups of the church are told to nominate a pastoral search committee, it is very likely that they will put together a list of nominees who probably will represent their group's interest but may or may not be committed to calling a Word-centered pastor. If pastoral search committee members do not share a commitment to the Word, bringing them together on a search committee will only serve to call attention to differences and it will do nothing to unify the church.

A second way that pastoral search committees are encouraged to pursue unity is by surveying the congregation to see what the congregation desires in their next pastor. These surveys ask everything from what style or philosophy of preaching the congregation desires to whether the congregation would like the next pastor to be introverted or extroverted.

Taking this type of survey can be inherently misleading

in the context of a pastoral search. If it is not properly administered, a survey conveys that the central goal of the survey-takers is to get an accurate read on what will most please the most people. Pleasing the majority, of course, is not the goal when finding the right pastor, so we should not imply so by polling for people's preferences. For one thing, it is possible, and it is ideal, for churches to enjoy biblical unity regardless of preferential unanimity. The leadership of the church ought to discourage partisanship and encourage unity whenever possible—and surveys do not mesh well with that goal.

Bible-believing Christians know that Christ is the head of the church (Colossians 1:18). He leads local churches through His Word. He alone is the One we should seek to please. So a pastoral search should be Word-centered from the get-go, not congregation-centered.

Thus the strategy of taking surveys can also lead to disunity. That doesn't mean a survey is always inappropriate. However, only a well-prepared, Word-centered survey should be used.

What is the Role of a Church Vote?

This is a good place to make a comment about church votes. Depending on the governance of your local church, you may or may not vote as a church about calling your next pastor. Good churches differ about whether there should be a vote. My intent here is not to argue the point one way or another, except to say that if you *do* vote, you ought not do so because you believe the church is a democracy. It is no such thing. Rather, better biblical reasons for voting would be because there are times when it is appropriate for church members to recognize together the call of God on a particular pastor, for them to agree corporately and pledge corporately their commitment to support and submit to their new God-given leader. You might also defend the practice of voting for a pastor on the basis that there is wisdom in many counselors, or because the Bible prizes unity.

However, beware of premises and actions that would inadvertently teach your congregation that church is a democracy in which you are seeking to discern the will of the people and to deliver accordingly.

So How *Do* We Promote and Preserve Unity?

What *is* the proper way for God's people to remain unified during a pastoral search? The first thing we need to recognize is that unity requires a center. For instance, if a group is going to unite physically, they must decide where. It's not enough to make some general declaration, "Let's get together." One needs to specify the place. You might say, "Let's meet at the Royal Blue Restaurant in Stillman Valley, Illinois."

Of course, the central goal for local churches is not essentially geographical in nature but *theological*. Churches are called to unite around the person and work of the Lord Jesus Christ as He is revealed in Scripture. So, the foundation for biblical unity is for a local church to establish again and again a Christocentric, biblical core focus.

As you study the New Testament, you quickly see that truth is the strategy for unifying God's people. The apostle

John says in 1 John 1:1–4 that Christ is central, that in focusing on Him, God's people have fellowship or share together; and as a result, their joy is made perfect.

Specific Strategies for Building Unity

Here are three specific and practical steps that your church can take to build unity.

> *Unity Building Exercise 1*. Review your church mission or purpose statement as well as central statements that define you as a church. Ask whoever is filling the pulpit to preach on relevant passages. Determine again as a whole congregation to be Word-centered in every aspect of the pastoral search process, rather than allowing pet preferences to eclipse the central focus.
>
> *Unity Building Exercise 2*. Develop a one- to two-page summary of the gospel and study it as a local church. If you ask people in your church, "What is the gospel?" you might be surprised at how people struggle to articulate it. It's at this point that your leaders can take a passage like 1 Corinthians 15:1–11 and study through it with the congregation. You can remind the congregation that the gospel extends beyond knowing we will be with Christ when we die, to continually shaping all of our relationships and governing everything we do as part of a local church.
>
> *Unity Building Exercise 3*. Teach through the book of Titus. For several reasons, Titus offers an ideal portion

of Scripture to study during a pastoral transition. The apostle Paul wrote the book of Titus for the purpose of equipping Titus to appoint elders.

Here are three elements to teaching Titus. First, review the qualifications for an elder listed in Titus 1:6–9. A church preparing to call a pastor is doing exactly what the apostle Paul wrote to Titus about—appointing an elder.

Second, teach the foundation of doctrine found in Titus. In 1:4, Paul addresses Titus as "my true son in our common faith" (NIV). From the beginning of the letter, Paul establishes that the basis for their unity—what they have in common—is their *faith*. Two of the most concentrated doctrinal passages found anywhere in Scripture are in Titus—in 2:11–14 and 3:3–8. The former, Titus 2:11–14, is a grand summary of how God's grace is at work in the life of His people while we wait for Christ's return. Titus 3:3–8 is a rich synopsis of the doctrine of salvation.

Finally, encourage the entire congregation to read through Titus several times and to meditate on its meaning. The book of Titus is a very manageable length. It is less than two pages in my Bible. Despite its brevity, the book of Titus is so doctrinally rich we could study it the rest of our lives and not exhaust its content.

How to Prepare a Survey

Earlier I warned that giving a survey can lead to disunity. But a Word-centered survey can help a search committee. There is certainly a place for gathering input from your congregation. Just remember, surveys are not neutral exercises. *All* surveys teach—one way or another. Whoever asks the questions leads the group. Take the phrasing of this question, for example: "Would you prefer to have a pastor who *never* preaches on money, or one who *does* often address financial matters from the pulpit?" The very asking of that question *teaches* that whether or not your next pastor challenges people about finances, his doing so ought to be a matter of congregational preference. A Word-centered pastoral search committee must take its cues from the Word first and foremost, and according to the Word, a pastor who preaches the whole counsel of God *must* challenge people about money.

It is possible to be Word-centered about anything, and surveys can be conducted in a Word-centered fashion. Surely, it is legitimate to ask questions in ways that presuppose and reaffirm the authority of God's Word. You might ask questions like this:

1. Given that our mission statement as a church is to "Glorify Christ and maximize our joy by making disciples," what might we tell pastoral candidates about how our church has been pursuing those goals and how we have most effectively fulfilled them in the last five years?
2. How do you think our church could improve in our efforts to fulfill our mission and purpose?
3. How committed are you to hearing the Word of God proclaimed in our church?
4. Can we tell pastoral candidates that you have reviewed our church doctrinal statement in the

past two months, and that you are committed to it?

You get the idea. Write questions in ways that presume biblical commitments and that remind and teach your people of what it is you are looking for in a pastor. That kind of survey can be an exercise for the congregation on a couple of fronts, not just building unity. Notice some survey questions are not just A. B. C. D. or *yes* or *no*; they can include short answers, as numbers 1 and 2 do above. And the feedback of your congregation to these sorts of questions will be valuable to you in assessing whether you are all on the same page. A Word-centered survey can in that way be a useful tool to let you know how unified your church is around Christ and His Word.

Doing a Self-Study and Church Profile

Early on in your search for a pastor, your church will want to do some sort of self-study and to build a profile of the church to be shared with prospective candidates and your church family. Reestablishing the central doctrinal commitments of your church is a good place to begin this process. If you have followed the steps recommended above, such as unity building exercises 1 and 2 (reviewing the gospel and the church's mission statement as a whole congregation), then include facts like that in the profile. You can write, "This is what our church is committed to unifying around in the days to come." You can delineate areas where you hope to grow and improve, and you can express the level of support among the congregation for a united front based on a central gospel focus.

Having clearly defined core commitments, you can also include in this profile:

- *A description of your community.* Include whatever will help candidates better understand the area and demographics where you live. Often the local chamber of commerce has helpful summaries. But you might also include newspaper clippings and favorite places to visit in your area.
- *An overview of your church,* including its history and where you are at presently. This could mention the strengths of your current position, as well as areas that need to be addressed as you move forward.
- *Two to three of your most recent annual reports.*
- *A multimedia presentation.* This could include pictures of your area and even video of one or two people in your church sharing what your local church has meant to them.

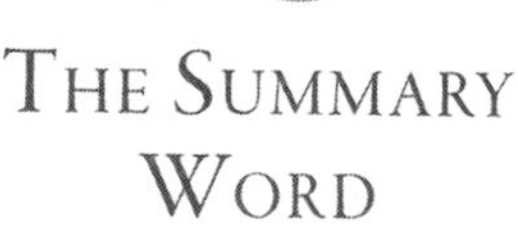

The Summary Word

In leading the church through the formation of a search committee and through the entire process of finding a pastor, you must be—and you must lead your church to be—centered on the Word, not driven and tossed with the whims and wish lists of individuals and groups. Nominating representatives from various groups within the congregation and surveying the congregation are *not* the best strategies for building unity. Indeed, if those are your first resorts, you may learn the hard way that they can create more disunity than unity. Your first step in building unity ought to be to establish again your theological center. For a church, this center should be the gospel, the person of Christ, and the sufficiency of His Word.

Recall from chapter 2 that the Bereans understood the need to be Word-centered: "They received the word with all eagerness, examining the Scriptures daily to see if these things were so" (Acts 17:11b). But there are still more lessons from the Bereans, especially for pastoral search committees. So we return to Berea in chapter 4.

TO CREATE A SEARCH COMMITTEE that is full of promise and has a high probability of success requires some thought and *planning*. No event is likely to be as crucial to the next 10 years of your church . . . as the shaping of this committee, so it warrants the best thinking possible—and that kind of thinking seldom comes in an instant.

Robert Dingman
In Search of a Leader

BEHOLD, I AM SENDING YOU out as sheep in the midst of wolves, so be wise as serpents and innocent as doves.

Matthew 10:16

4

More Lessons from the Bereans

I didn't get to listen to the whole thing," confessed Laura, "but I liked what I did hear." It was meeting number thirteen for the pastoral search committee of Calvary Church. (They knew it was the thirteenth meeting because they were keeping track.) The committee was interested in Doug Baxter as a possibility to become their next pastor. At meeting number twelve, they had all agreed to download and listen to one of his sermons prior to the next meeting.

No one on the committee could blame Laura for not finding time. She worked full-time, was actively involved in the church children's ministry, and her boys were in the middle of soccer season. Actually, many on the committee wondered how she managed to juggle everything and still even show up at their meetings.

Others on the committee had trouble finding time to listen to the sermon download. In fact, by this stage in the process (meeting number thirteen?!), the whole committee was motivated to move on with Baxter, even if some of them had not yet been able to review the candidate's sermons. Months earlier they had reason to hope they might be on the home stretch when a prior pastoral candidate had come to preach. Several in the congregation voiced concerns about the candidate's doctrinal views. It was in an area that most of the search committee didn't really care about, and they were convinced that it wasn't a big deal. In the end it turned out that it *was* a big deal to the candidate, who withdrew his name.

For the pastoral search committee, the whole ordeal had been a train wreck, and they were anxious to put the entire search behind them. Now they were tired, and not every committee member was ready to listen to messages from the latest candidate.

Tired and Feeling the Pressure

Not only had the PSC grown weary of PSC-ing, but the committee members were feeling increasing pressure from the congregation to submit another name to the elders soon. Meeting number thirteen seemed like it would be The One when they could finally agree . . . and so far, so good. They had sailed through the agenda. The committee chairman, Dean Ferguson, had opened the meeting in prayer. The next order of business had been to postpone or cancel the proposed visit from their district denominational leader, given that they already were zeroing in on a new candidate.

The district official had offered to come discuss with them the doctrinal questions that were a source of the congregational concerns about the last candidate. That seemed a little like overkill to the committee, since that former candidate had withdrawn his name. He was out of the picture. It was time to move forward.

The last point on the agenda for the meeting had been this discussion of Doug Baxter's preaching—which is why Laura had explained that she was able to listen to only part of the sermon during her time in the car that day. Dean spoke next. "Listen, I liked the sermon a lot. I'm no theology guru, and I'm not really the kind of guy who gets into in-depth evaluation stuff, but what I do appreciate is that he just seems real down-to-earth and able to relate to his listeners. As for the theological part, we all know that the seminary he attended is where *two of our previous pastors* attended."

The discussion continued from there. Joe Hawthorne had been in charge of calling references. He had contacted one of them just for a few minutes before the meeting, and the feedback had been very positive. Joe concluded, "You know, I found myself agreeing with the reference. From everything I've seen and heard, I just like the guy. I think he'd make a good pastor." Everyone nodded in agreement.

Of course, two committee members weren't nodding because they weren't even in attendance, due to scheduling conflicts. The missing persons had sent word through Joe, however, that they were in favor of going on to the next step in pursuing Doug Baxter.

Can You Spot the Errors?

Growing up, I remember children's magazines that had pencil drawings containing intentionally hidden errors. In the picture, there would be cars with square wheels, or pigs with horns, and the idea was that you had to find as many errors as possible. If you studied the picture for any time at all, most of the errors were obvious.

Looking at the picture I sketched above of this fictitious Calvary Church's pastoral search committee meeting, maybe you could spot the errors. One difference between this sketch and those in children's magazines is that the errors are real. Pastoral search committees and entire congregations do often commit these mistakes. If you drive down the highway, you won't see cars with square wheels. But pastoral search committees do frequently make these foundational mistakes.

And another difference between the magazine sketches and Calvary's PSC is that the consequences of overlooking an error-riddled pastoral search process are far more serious—potentially devastating to a church. The difficulty isn't in spotting these kinds of errors in *other* churches. The hard part is guarding against them so they will not occur in your own church.

Not even the best-intentioned search committee is above making mistakes. How can you avoid these common pitfalls in your pastoral search process? Let's review what we've found so far:

- We should recognize that we cannot succeed in a search for a pastor in our own strength, and this should motivate us to pray (chapter 1).
- We should follow the example of the Bereans, who pleased God and were also effective leaders. The first quality to notice about the Bereans is that they were Word-centered (chapter 2).
- The basic strategy for pursuing unity should be to stress the gospel's significance as the center around which your church will unite (chapter 3).

More Qualities a Church Needs

Let's revisit the Berean model and explore still other qualities that a church should emulate in its search for a new pastor.

Humble and Teachable

Not only were the Bereans Word-centered, but they were also humble and teachable. Luke says that the Bereans "received the message with all eagerness" (Acts 17:11). The word translated "eagerness" might also be translated "zeal." The Bereans did not assume that they already understood all they needed to know about God's Word. They recognized that they needed to learn from men like Paul and Silas.

There is a steep learning curve when you call a pastor.

Even for churches that have many mature believers, there is always a need to be teachable and to learn more about what is going on currently in Christendom. The good news is that for those willing to learn, there are many opportunities to receive the message with eagerness—especially in our day of technological advances in communications, news-sharing, and networking.

Unfortunately, humility and teachability can become an uneasy stretch for many pastoral search committees. Some of this has to do with the kinds of people who generally end up comprising a pastoral search committee. No doubt, some of the most capable and gifted people will be spearheading the pastoral search, and as is often the case with these sorts (like the guy writing this book), they will also be independent, strong-willed, and even a little hard-headed (in a Christian sort of way!).

This is okay, provided that these people *recognize* that they defend strong opinions and that there is much to learn about calling a pastor. But if a person does not think he or she needs to learn—and to learn a great deal—about calling a pastor, then he or she will be much more of a hindrance to the pastoral search than a help.

Recall that the pastoral search committee at Calvary Church dismissed the idea of having a denominational leader come in to help them understand the issues and ensuing conflict that had led to a previous candidate withdrawing his name. Similarly, many if not most pastoral search committees do not take advantage of the resources available to them from their denominational leaders. Accepting input from beyond your local assembly doesn't require that you must agree with everything the representative says. An outsider looking in brings both advantages and drawbacks—his perspective may not be as "in the know" and nuanced about details of the church's makeup and history, but by very virtue of coming from the outside, he will bring some objectivity and a broader scope to the table. There is no way that you can stay abreast of things on your own.

Be humble and teachable and learn from others. (For more on this point, see question 4 under "Frequently Asked Questions": "We have a number of experienced people in our church; can we do the search without any outside help?")

I have already stressed this next point in chapter 1 (on prayer). But let me say it again: An attitude of self-reliance will destroy your search for a pastor. Not only does this mentality lead to prayerlessness, but it also promotes an unwillingness among the pastoral search committee to learn from others. Be like the Bereans. Don't assume you already understand everything. Be willing to be taught.

Discerning

Humility and teachability are not *gullibility*. Being humble and teachable doesn't mean that you naïvely believe everything people tell you. Luke also commends the Bereans because they examined the Scripture for themselves. The word translated "examining" was often used in the first century for the context of legal transactions. The Bereans judiciously scrutinized the Scriptures, to verify whether what Paul said was true. While a pastoral search committee should be motivated to learn a great deal in a short period of time, they cannot afford to be naïve. Indeed, they will need to carefully examine pastoral candidates in every way to see if they are a good fit.

The Bible consistently emphasizes the need for discernment (Proverbs 14:8, 15; Matthew 10:16; Philippians 1:9–11; Romans 12:1–2). Proverbs 26:10 warns, "Like an archer who wounds everyone is one who hires a passing fool or drunkard."

And it is not always immediately obvious that someone is a fool. Again, pointing back to the example at the beginning, it won't work to make a quick reference call the afternoon before a meeting. On the surface, Joe may have appeared to meet his obligations responsibly, but his actions and assumptions may actually end up doing more damage to the overall effectiveness of the search than Laura's failure to listen to the entire sermon!

Keep in mind that a Berean-like pastoral search committee isn't evaluating only the candidates! It is imperative for the PSC and the church to examine the church itself as well. What sort of candidate is needed for your church? Who will fit well within your community? Is your community a place where a particular candidate is likely to stay over a long period of time? God *may* lead someone to move from Miami to the Upper Midwest. But a discerning church ought to think carefully about whether or not it is a wise decision to proceed with a particular candidate who will have to travel a great distance culturally and geographically to become the next pastor.

Specifically, even for practical and legal reasons, you must be sure to do the following:

- *Check references.* It is mind-boggling how many churches do not check references!
- *Do a credit check.* You do not need to require that candidates have Triple-A credit. But, if there are significant financial issues then the church needs to be aware.
- *Do a thorough criminal background check.*

Diligent

I have already argued that the eagerness or zeal of the Bereans indicates they were humble and teachable. Their eagerness also fueled their diligence. They were willing to work hard to understand what they were being taught. Verse 11 says they examined the Scriptures *daily*.

The longer I serve as a pastor, the more I appreciate the sacrifices church members make in order to serve. I cannot tell you how many meetings I have attended with people who skipped their evening meal after work so they could join us. I have been out past midnight in countless elder meetings where the participants knew full well they would have to be at work by 5:30 or 6:00 the next morning. My wife and I are raising four children, so we have some idea of the demands faced by busy families.

That is a lot to ask—but it is crucial that those involved in a pastoral search be committed to working very hard! No matter how busy and overwhelmed you already may be, the reality is that you will not be successful in a pastoral search apart from a lot of really hard work. Indeed, one of the main reasons that many churches fail in their pastoral search is that they aren't willing to do the necessary hard work.

Those on the Calvary Church pastoral search committee, for example, ought to have been exhorting one another about diligence and follow-through. If people do not follow through on assignments, they may need admonishment about the nature of the obligations they agreed to fulfill. If people are truly too busy to follow through on assignments, they may need to step aside and remove themselves from the pastoral search committee. As much as we all would like to be able to juggle everything responsibly, too much is at stake in a pastoral search to risk making uninformed decisions because someone did not do his job.

Excellent Crisis Managers

Paul and Silas traveled to Berea only after leaving Thessalonica because of a riot (Acts 17:5–9). Those who caused the riot soon followed Paul to Berea, and things became dangerous. The Bereans responded by hustling Paul out of town. Some of them traveled part of the distance with him to Athens.

You should try to picture in your mind all that this risky escape plan meant for the Bereans who had accepted the gospel. Theirs was a hostile world, and being caught with Paul at this point could well have meant death. Those who decided to accompany Paul for part of the journey did not enjoy modern communications; they couldn't text their families periodically to let them know they were okay. Still, by God's grace, they were able to work out a plan for

Paul to get out of town, and for the gospel to go forward.

Advancing the gospel in a fallen world is never safe nor easy. When you face difficult circumstances looking for a pastor, one thing you should not be is surprised. Opposition is to be expected. Choose search committee members who will not falter in a time of trouble (Proverbs 24:10), but who will focus on Christ and continue on, enduring the hard work and the temporary afflictions for the joy set before them (Hebrews 12:1–3).

In the example, the congregation of Calvary Church had divided over the theology of another candidate. The candidate then withdrew his name. Setbacks such as this happen often. It leaves a bad taste in people's mouths, and some have a hard time getting past it. But it does happen. During your pastoral search, *expect* your church to run into obstacles and crises. Don't be surprised at the painful trials you suffer during a pastoral search (1 Peter 4:12). Rather, determine to be a church that prayerfully and biblically perseveres. Carefully evaluate your options. Make careful and wise choices.

The Summary Word

As a church in general, and especially as a pastoral search committee, determine to be like the Bereans. Establish the following values as priorities for your church during a pastoral search:

1. *Passionately Word-centered.* Center your search on the gospel.
2. *Humble and teachable.* Read outside resources. Take advantage of denominational leaders' insight and other helps available.
3. *Discerning.* Be as wise as serpents and as innocent as doves (Matthew 10:16).
4. *Diligent.* Don't justify a lack of follow-through by telling one another that you are all very busy.
5. *Persevering.* Be prepared to face a serious crisis or two, and determine to work through them biblically and prayerfully.

As a search committee, hold to these five values, and keep one another accountable to maintaining them during your pastoral search.

Part 2

Judge, Lest You Be Judged

IN MATTHEW 7:1 JESUS SAYS, "Do not judge, or you too will be judged." That verse in mind, it may surprise you that I have given this part the title, "Judge, Lest You Be Judged." After all, Matthew 7:1 may have surpassed John 3:16 as the most well-known verse in the Bible. Even people who are not Christians quote this verse.

To be sure, Jesus taught that there is a kind of wrong judging. If we make evaluations about people without first bringing ourselves under the same standard, then this is a serious offense (Matthew 7:1–5). In implementing Jesus' exhortation, however, we need to be careful that we do not throw biblical discernment out with the bathwater of hypocrisy. Make no mistake. In order to call a pastor you will need discernment to rightly judge or evaluate the candidate. So the goal in this section is to equip you to judge or evaluate in the right way, lest you be accountable to God for not wisely leading your church forward.

IF THE CHURCH IS TO BE CALLED a flock, the Minister is the pastor to "seek that which is lost—to strengthen the diseased—to heal the sick—to bring again that which was driven away"; in a word, to shepherd the flock in all the exercises of tenderness, consideration, and care, that belong to this endearing character.

Charles Bridges
The Christian Ministry with an Inquiry into the Causes of Its Inefficiency

Pay careful attention to yourselves and to all the flock, in which the Holy Spirit has made you overseers, to care for the church of God, which he obtained with his own blood.

Acts 20:28

5

Look for a Shepherd

When I was growing up, the major celebration of my hometown, Keosauqua, Iowa, was "Sheep Empire Day." Let me tell you, it was a gala event, meant to celebrate the sheep industry in Southeast Iowa. The centerpiece of the celebration was a parade, and everyone who entered a parade float had to *think sheep and shepherding.* "Miss Sheep Queen"—selected on the basis of social poise and her family's involvement in the mutton industry, not always an easy combination to find—would ride in a convertible. Floats featured slogans like "Frank's Phillips 66 Wants Ewe To Stop By" or "Pete's Dairy Freeze Says, 'Come Baa-Baa-Back for Ice Cream.'" The Jaycees would serve mutton at the fairgrounds after the parade.

On Tending Sheep

They no longer celebrate Sheep Empire Day in Keosauqua, but I assure you that the "Sheep Empire" mindset is relevant for every pastoral search committee. Those on a pastoral search committee need to *think sheep and shepherding.* Like the Keosauquites did for Sheep Empire Day, you as a pastoral search committee need to reflect on the imagery of tending sheep.

The reason is straightforward. The overarching metaphor the New Testament gives of a pastor is that he needs to be a shepherd. Indeed, the term "pastor" *means* "shepherd." The image of shepherding is used throughout the Scriptures to refer to biblical leadership (Isaiah 53:6–7; Jeremiah 3:15; 23:1–4; Matthew 9:35–38; Luke 15:3–7). Christ Himself is called the Good Shepherd (John 10:11), the Chief Shepherd (1 Peter 5:4), and the Great Shepherd (Hebrews 13:20).

The Kind of Shepherd to Call

So my aim in this chapter is to help you have a "Sheep Empire Day" mentality in that your pastoral search should be permeated with shepherd-oriented thinking. You ought to be biblically biased about the sort of man you should call—biased for him to have shepherd-like qualities. Here are seven qualities of a good shepherd for the church:

1. The Shepherd Will Lead with Exemplary Character

The New Testament makes it clear that a foundational qualification for being a shepherd or being a pastor is godly character. The apostle Peter insists that shepherds shouldn't lord it over those entrusted to them, but that they ought to be examples to the flock (1 Peter 5:3). Both 1 Timothy 3:2–7 and Titus 1:6–8 focus on character requirements for pastoral ministry. The two passages are remarkably similar,[1] so here I will summarize only Titus 1:6–8.

> If anyone is above reproach, the husband of one wife, and his children are believers and not open to the charge of debauchery or insubordination. For an overseer, as God's steward, must be above reproach. He must not be arrogant or quick-tempered or a drunkard or violent or greedy for gain, but hospitable, a lover of good, self-controlled, upright, holy, and disciplined.

An elder must be blameless, the husband of but one wife, a man whose children believe and are not open to the charge of being wild and disobedient. Since an overseer is entrusted with God's work, he must be blameless—not overbearing, not quick-tempered, not given to drunkenness, not violent, not pursuing dishonest gain. Rather he must be hospitable, one who loves what is good, who is "self-controlled, upright, holy, and disciplined."

"Above reproach" is the overarching qualification. Reputation *is* important; and we cannot soil the testimony of Christ's church by appointing leaders who are *not* above reproach.

"The husband of one wife" does not mean that one must be married in order to be an elder—just as the ensuing verses do not require that one must necessarily have a family to be an elder. Rather, the passage mandates that pastors should be above reproach in their emotional and physical relationships—morally pure and faithful to their wives if they are married, and morally pure if they are single. Churches should also plan to question pastors about how they are doing with the unique temptations of the Internet.

The apostle Paul adds that this spiritual leader has children who "are believers and not open to the charge of debauchery or insubordination." A man who allows his children to run wild is not qualified. If he is not leading his home, if his children are not aligned under his authority, then *he is not qualified to shepherd a flock*. Notice the parallel passage in 1 Timothy 3:4–5: "He must manage his own household well, with all dignity keeping his children submissive, for if someone does not know how to manage his own household, how will he care for God's church?"

In outlining character qualifications for Titus, Paul stresses a number of things that godly shepherds ought *not* be. A shepherd should not be "arrogant." In the original language, the word for "arrogant" is an antonym of *gentle*, *kind*, and *gracious*. A shepherd should not be quick-tempered or inclined to sudden, uncontrollable anger. Anger is *not* always wrong. But a person who is known for flying off the handle all the time is *not* someone you ought to call as your next pastor. A biblical shepherd is not a drunkard, nor under the control of other addictions. A pastor should never be a bully or fighter—not literally, nor in arguments. "He who loves a quarrel loves sin" (Proverbs

17:19 NIV). Nor should a biblical shepherd ever be characterized as "greedy" or "materialistic."

Rather, seek for your church a pastor who is known for the biblical characteristic of *hospitality*, someone who likes to invest in and share his life with other people. This doesn't mean that you get to have copies of all his house keys, nor that pastors aren't allowed to let their phones ring through to voice mail. It doesn't mean that pastors must all practice hospitality in the same ways. But, Christians *are* called to share life together in community, and a pastor ought especially to exemplify a hospitable spirit for the sake of his flock.

Your next pastor should be a "lover of good, self-controlled, upright, holy, and disciplined." *Disciplined* appears in verse 8, the only time in the New Testament. It carries the idea of the discipline exhibited by an athlete, striving consistently and sacrificially toward excellence and victory. Ministry is hard work. The qualified shepherd's life should reflect dignity and a moral purity.

2. The Shepherd Will Feed His Flock the Word of God

Like our perfect example, Jesus Christ, godly shepherds lead the flock into the green pastures of God's Word. That shepherding and teaching the Word are inextricably linked is seen in Ephesians 4:11–12: "And he gave the apostles, the prophets, the evangelists, *the pastors and teachers*, to equip the saints for the work of ministry, for building up the body of Christ" (emphasis added).

In verse 11, it is more accurate to translate the phrase

"pastors and teachers" by hyphenating the two words so that it reads "pastor-teachers."[2] In Ephesians 4, the thought is that the victorious Christ ascended to the right hand of the Father in order that the Holy Spirit might gift some to be pastor- or shepherd-teachers in local churches.

The essence of feeding the flock is preaching the Word. Some resources for pastoral search committees downplay the importance of preaching. They say something like, "The new pastor will be doing a lot more than preaching, so we can't place all the attention on the candidate's preaching." Yet just the opposite is true—the candidate's preaching philosophy and capabilities ought to be *paramount* in your evaluation of his fitness to shepherd your church.

It is true that a pastor is called upon to wear a lot of hats. The nature of the role requires a minister who is versatile, flexible, both willing and able to attend to all kinds of needs in his flock and the surrounding community. Therefore some would ask, "Is it possible to go overboard and major too much on the importance of preaching? Sure, preaching's a big deal. But does the way a candidate handles the Word *really* count much more than everything?"

A great place to find an answer to that question is in the epistles to Timothy and Titus. Paul wrote 2 Timothy for the purpose of reminding Timothy where his focus ought to be in the ministry.[3] In the same section where Paul tells Timothy that all Scripture is "God-breathed" (2 Timothy 3:16), he immediately states that the significance and purpose of that inspiration of Scripture is that God's man—

most directly referring to preachers—might be equipped for every good work.

He follows this up with another exhortation to Timothy: "I charge you in the presence of God and of Christ Jesus, who is to judge the living and the dead, and by his appearing and his kingdom: preach the word; be ready in season and out of season; reprove, rebuke, and exhort, with complete patience and teaching" (2 Timothy 4:1–2).

For Paul, the most immediate application of the doctrine of the inspiration of Scripture is that the Word should be preached. In reference to this passage, John Piper agrees: "There ARE other things to do in the ministry, as these letters to Timothy show. And we must do them to be found faithful. But none of them is treated as solemnly and forcefully as this one simple exhortation from the apostle: "Preach the Word."[4]

Paul tells Timothy to devote himself to the public reading of Scripture, to preaching and teaching (1 Timothy 4:13). He also instructs Titus, who is appointing elders in Crete (Titus 1:5), to be Word-centered: "But as for you, teach what accords with sound doctrine" (Titus 2:1). In listing the qualifications for the office of elder in Titus 1:6–8, Paul focuses on character qualities. But in terms of what elders should *do,* Paul instructs Titus to look for more: "He must hold firm to the trustworthy word as taught, so that he may be able to give instruction in sound doctrine and also to rebuke those who contradict it" (Titus 1:9). In 1 Timothy 3:2, Paul simply adds that elders must be "able to teach."

Keep in mind the pastor will feed the congregation in other settings besides the pulpit. Your next pastor must be able to analyze a problem in the flock and give direction for the future. You are looking for a pastor who can counsel people from the Word of God. This doesn't mean that he must devote *all* his time to counseling. But he does need to be gifted in enabling the flock to see how the Word of God comes to bear on the whole spectrum of diverse situations they will face in life. This might include marriage counseling, premarital counseling, counseling people struggling with addictions, or bearing up those who have been devastated by unimaginable tragedy.

3. The Shepherd Will Desire to Know Your Church and Community

Jesus said, "I am the good shepherd. I know my own and my own know me" (John 10:14). Following the Lord's example, Christlike shepherds make it their goal to *know* the flock intimately. They are involved in the lives of their sheep. Look for a pastor who demonstrates a desire to be a student of your community and your congregation. He should want to study and learn the depth and breadth of the needs. He should seek to know the individual and corporate stories of your community so that he can lead in a personal and intimate way, guiding knowledgeably within that specific context.

It is necessary to insert here a word of warning. While you ought to be searching for a pastor who is motivated to know your congregation in a very close and personal way, that expectation does *not* require that a pastor be best friends with everybody. If your church grows numerically at all, such an unlikely standard will soon become an impossible one.

4. The Shepherd Will Sacrificially Love Your Church

Jesus said that the good shepherd lays down his life for the sheep (John 10:11). Having grown up on a farm, this image has always amazed me. We certainly *cared about* our livestock. But it *never* would have crossed our minds *to die for* one of our animals. Indeed, depending on the supply and demand of bacon and beef, it often worked the other way around—they would die for us! The stunning beauty of Christ as our shepherd is that He laid down His life for His flock.

His sacrifice is not only the basis for our salvation, but also an example that those in His church ought to follow (1 Peter 2:21–25). Pastors in particular are to love their congregations so deeply that they would indeed *die* for them. Your church doesn't need a hired hand who is going to run like the wind at the first sign of a wolf (John 10:12). Your church needs a *good* shepherd who will lay down his life for his sheep.

Keep this truth about self-sacrificing in mind if the pastor you call is already shepherding a flock somewhere else. The sort of pastor you are looking for loves his flock enough to die for them. If God does call him to another context, then he will feel as though he is being torn in half. This phenomenon doesn't mean God never calls a pastor to shepherd another flock, nor that you should feel responsible for the grief of saying good-bye. But it does mean that you ought to be very sensitive to how difficult it will be (and that even the difficulty is a healthy indicator of the kind of shepherd-sheep relationship described by Jesus).

5. The Shepherd Will Guard Your Flock from Dangers

For sheep, the valley of the shadow of death is never far away. There are always predators who threaten to creep in and kill the sheep (Acts 20:28–31; Jude 4). All the while, we are in constant peril. The Evil One prowls around like a roaring lion, seeking to devour (1 Peter 5:8).

Biblical shepherds understand the stakes and are alert to dangers their churches may face. They stay apprised of trends in theology and are on the lookout for those teachings that may undermine the doctrinal foundations.

6. The Shepherd Will Point Your Flock toward a Biblically Positive Vision

Psalm 23 does *not* say that the Lord leads us into the Gobi Desert. Rather, He leads us into green pastures, and we will dwell in His house forever. No pastor who has a negative view of the future can lead his flock forward. Look for a pastor who sees great opportunities for how your church can be used in the work of the kingdom, and who encourages you to pursue those opportunities. The key to a pastor's ability to lead his flock forward is that he himself has his eyes on Christ—His future return, His eternal presence, and the promise of a new earth, where there is no more death, mourning, crying, or pain (Revelation 21–22).

Your next shepherd must encourage your people again and again that they have a living hope through the resurrection of Christ from the dead and an inheritance that will never perish, spoil, or fade (see 1 Peter 1:3–9).

7. The Shepherd Cares for the Lambs Who Stray

Biblical shepherds feel a responsibility to look for lost sheep. They understand that there is great rejoicing in heaven over sinners who come back to the fold (Luke 15:3–7). Clowney summarizes:

> Jesus the Lord came to gather his scattered sheep. He told his disciples that whoever did not gather with him scattered abroad. Faithful shepherds do more than care for the sheep in the fold; like the Savior, they are seeking shepherds. They witness to the Gentile world in which they are now "scattered" for the sake of their mission.[5]

Shepherds understand that if one of the lambs does wander from the flock, then eternity is at stake. They pursue strays with the knowledge that "whoever brings back a sinner from his wandering will save his soul from death and will cover a multitude of sins" (James 5:20b).

The Summary Word

As I said in the introduction, no pastor will perfectly embody all of these qualities. But look for a shepherd who exhibits most of them and strives to do so increasingly.

Having said that, the longer I reflect on the imagery of God's people being sheep who need a shepherd, the more I appreciate the richness of this metaphor. We are vulnerable. We do easily stray. We do need a leader who knows us personally. While this need for a shepherd is one ultimately only Christ can meet, the Lord chooses to work through undershepherds who tend the flock. This being the case, it is imperative that your church calls a shepherd who is himself called by Christ.

Like sheep, we need a shepherd who will lead us into green pastures. We know that those pastures contain God's Word. Beyond having the shepherd feed us, though, we need to understand the specific ingredients the pastor includes. Knowing this will help us to evaluate various candidates. This is the subject of the next chapter.

Notes

1. William D. Mounce, *Pastoral Epistles,* Word Biblical Commentary, vol. 46 (Nashville: Nelson, 2000), 155.
2. S. D. F. Salmond, "Ephesians," *The Expositor's Greek New Testament,* ed. Robertson Nicoll (Grand Rapids: Eerdmans, 1990), 330.
3. Gordon D. Fee, *1 and 2 Timothy, Titus,* New International Biblical Commentary, vol. 13 (Peabody, Mass.: Hendrickson, 1988), 12–14.

4. John Piper, *Advice to Pastors: Preach the Word* (Desiring God Ministries, 1996, accessed September 24 2004); available from http://www.desiringgod.org/library/topics/leadership/advice_preach.html. Piper points out that there are five ways in this passage in which Paul intensifies the command: 1. "I solemnly charge you"; 2. "in the presence of God"; 3. "and of Christ Jesus" (both the Father and the Son have a great concern in this matter); 4. "who is to judge the living and the dead"; 5. "and by his appearing and his kingdom."
5. Edmund Clowney, *The Message of 1 Peter*, ed. John R.W. Stott, *The Bible Speaks Today* (Downers Grove, Ill.: InterVarsity, 1988), 201.

LIVE UNDER THE CLEAREST, distinct, convincing teaching that possibly you can procure. There is an unspeakable difference as to the edification of the hearers, between a judicious, clear, distinct, and skillful preacher, and one that is ignorant, confused, general, dry, and only scrapeth together a . . . mingle-mangle of some undigested saying to fill up the hour with.

Richard Baxter
The Practical Works of Richard Baxter

ONE OF THE FIRST STEPS to a recovering of authentic Christian preaching is to stop saying, “I prefer expository preaching.” Rather, we should define exactly what we mean when we say “preach.”

Albert Mohler
He Is Not Silent

I CHARGE YOU IN THE PRESENCE of God and of Christ Jesus, who is to judge the living and the dead, and by his appearing and his kingdom: preach the word; be ready in season and out of season; reprove, rebuke, and exhort, with complete patience and teaching. For the time is coming when people will not endure sound teaching, but having itching ears they will accumulate for themselves teachers to suit their own passions, and will turn away from listening to the truth and wander off into myths.

2 Timothy 4:1–4

6

The Recipe for a Biblical Meal "Done Just Right"

I really like eating at Outback Steakhouse. Each time I order a steak there, the server asks me how I would like it cooked. I always respond "medium," and invariably the person taking my order says, "'Medium' means warm throughout, with pink in the middle and just a touch of red." As a certified Outback expert, I then say something profound, like, "Okay."

I am not alone in my appreciation for Outback. Chances are, if you live near a major American city (they're in every state except North Dakota), there is an Outback Steakhouse, even though we are a long way from Australia. I think part of their success is due to that little conversation that takes place every time you order a steak from them. Outback *defines* their terms. They make sure that when you order a steak from them, you know what you are getting. It's done just right.

What Is Expository Preaching?

In chapter 5 we noted that your next pastor should be a good shepherd who will feed his flock the Word of God. To pursue that goal, you need to understand the *kind of* preaching that best ensures you will receive a biblical message. In this section, I want to explain why the type of preaching known as "expository preaching" is the type that best ensures communication of a truly biblical message. And if you are going to order an "expository special," then you need to make sure that you as a committee agree (with "Outback precision") on what the term "expository preaching" even means.

Some have argued that because there are *so many different* definitions of expository preaching, we simply ought to do away with the term. While I agree that different definitions do present problems, the solution I would propose is that, rather than getting rid of the term "expository preaching," we should instead agree about the definition. Use my Outback Steakhouse example. Suppose that when I ordered a steak, the dialogue went something like this:

Chris: "I would like to order an Outback Special, and I would like the steak cooked 'medium.'"

Outback Waiter: "I am sorry, but in collecting definitions from fifty different steakhouses, we have found that none of them means the same thing by 'medium,' so we have done away with any labels."

Where would that leave me—besides *hungry*? The bottom line is that if I am going to order a steak, then I need some wording that specifies exactly what I am after. And if you are going to order up some biblical preaching, then you will need to agree on definitions that specify exactly what you're seeking. Whether you use the term "expository preaching" or not, it is critical that your search committee agrees with precision about what they are looking for in the preaching of your next pastor.

What Is the Goal of Preaching?

Before I talk about expository preaching in particular, let's fix in our minds the ultimate goal for preaching. In the simplest form, the goal of preaching is for truth to nourish God's people.

Chart 1. The Basic Goal of Preaching

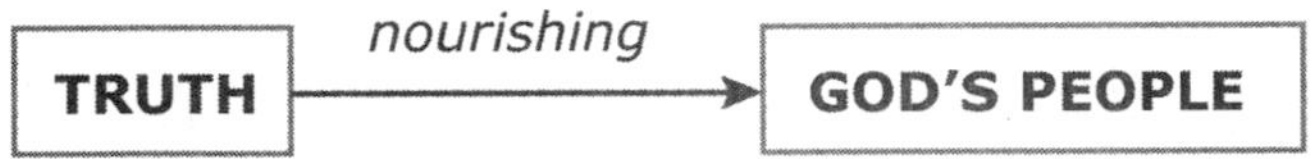

Remember, it is the preached gospel of God's Word that brings life. Faith comes from hearing, and hearing through the Word of Christ (Romans 10:17). It is in hearing the Word that we see our need for the glorious news of Christ and are born again to new life in Him (John 3:5–7; 2 Corinthians 5:16–17; Titus 3:5).

After God uses the proclaimed Word to give life, He continues to nourish His people through it as they are reproved, corrected, and trained in righteousness (2 Timothy 3:16).

Preaching where truth nourishes life could happen in many different forms. To be honest, you wouldn't even need to have your Bibles with you. Now, don't stop reading right here, because this is *certainly not* what I want to happen. The point is it would be possible for a preacher to stand up and simply share a single truth and then talk about its significance for life. Such an approach might work for black-and-white areas like "Don't kill people." Difficulties would show up in murky or controversial areas. If the preacher simply stood up in the pulpit and said something that our culture doesn't readily accept, then people could rightly respond, "Says *who*?"

In order for preaching to be consistently right and authoritative, there needs to be confidence that the message proclaimed flows out of the intended meaning of God's Word. Your people don't need just another man's slant on life. They need a Word from God. While it is possible for preaching to take other forms, the kind of preaching that best ensures that the truth is proclaimed is expository preaching.

When you think of expository preaching, you may picture a particular preacher. In fact, you may already be thinking, "Oh, great. This guy thinks everyone should preach the same way as [so-and-so]." That is not the case. Expository preaching is more about a commitment than it is about a particular style. On the contrary—a commitment to expository preaching can lead to a variety of styles, because God's Word has variety and God's men are unique. Haddon Robinson shares this insight: "If sermons are truly biblical, we would not expect them to resemble one another like cookies on a baking sheet. . . . Sermons built on the Scriptures will assume varied forms just as the literature of the Bible makes use of many different genres."[1]

The dictionary defines "exposition" as the "setting forth of meaning or purpose." In the case of expository preaching, the goal is to set forth the meaning and life-changing purpose of the Bible. Expository preaching moves from what a passage *meant* in its original context to what it *means* today. This is done in such a way that the listener knows that this is a Word from God.

A Useful Definition

If you were not on a pastoral search committee, what I have developed above might be a satisfying enough explanation of expository preaching. The fact remains that you are going to have to evaluate many different sermons in the days to come. For that reason, we need to go deeper in understanding what expository preaching is. Let's establish more clearly what is meant by the term "expository preaching"—here's how Haddon Robinson defines it:

> Expository preaching is the communication of a biblical concept, derived from and transmitted through a historical, grammatical, and literary study of a passage in its context, which the Holy Spirit first applies to the personality and experience of the preacher, then through the preacher, applies to the hearers.[2]

Understanding the concept of what distinguishes expository preaching from lesser alternatives is key to calling your next preacher. The hard work you invest now to study and understand why expository preaching is significantly different and preferable to other forms will eventually pay off—for the benefit of your whole church, and for many years to come.

See if the diagram on the next page helps. It divides Haddon Robinson's definition of expository preaching into five stages or steps for preparing an expository sermon. *My aim is to help you understand the essence of expository preaching.* Start with box #1 and follow the arrows to work through the definition as a whole concept.

Understanding the Five Steps of Preparing an Expository Sermon

Each of the five boxes in Chart 2 is very important. Combined, they make up the essence of expository preaching. To understand these five steps, let me give you an example. To keep it simple (and to remind you of ground already covered), I will focus again on the Bereans in Acts 17:10–12.

> *The brothers immediately sent Paul and Silas away by night to Berea, and when they arrived they went into the Jewish synagogue. Now these Jews were more noble than those in Thessalonica; they received the word with all eagerness, examining the Scriptures daily to see if these things were so. Many of them therefore believed, with not a few Greek women of high standing as well as men.* (Acts 17:10–12)

Chart 2

Five Steps of Preparing an Expository Sermon*

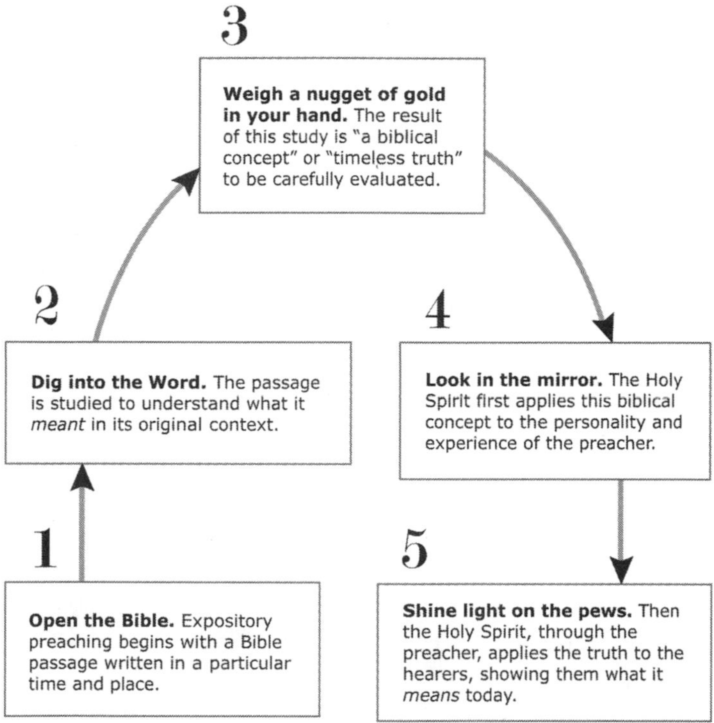

* The wording of these five steps comes directly from the definition of expository preaching by Haddon Robinson in *Biblical Preaching,* 2nd ed. (Baker), 21. The concept of the five-step approach comes from Chris Brauns.

Step one: *Open the Bible.* Remember, expository preaching begins with a Bible passage written in a particular time and place. Acts 17:10–12 is taken from the book of Acts. Acts was written by Dr. Luke in the first century, and it describes the beginning of the church. Summed up into a single sentence, the book of Acts is about how the church begins as the Word spreads in the power of the Holy Spirit.3

Step two: *Dig into the Word.* The preacher studies the passage to understand what it *meant* in its original context. In this section of Acts, Luke describes the spread of the Word during the apostle Paul's second missionary journey. Acts 9 tells of Paul's dramatic conversion. In Acts 13, the church commissions Paul and Barnabas for the first mission trip; and in Acts 16, Paul receives the Macedonian call and goes into Europe. He travels first to Philippi, then to Thessalonica, then to Berea—the setting for this passage, Acts 17:10–12. Paul faces opposition in Thessalonica; and this is contrasted with the more positive response modeled by the Bereans. What did the Bereans do that pleased our heavenly Father? They received the preached Word from Paul and Barnabas with eagerness. They carefully studied the Scriptures for themselves.

Step three: *Weigh a nugget of gold in your hand.* From this study arises "a biblical concept" or "timeless truth" to be carefully evaluated. We distill from this passage a "timeless truth." Here it is: *God is pleased with people who eagerly receive the preached Word and diligently study it for themselves.*

Step four: *Look in the mirror.* The Holy Spirit first applies this biblical concept to the personality and experience of the preacher. The above truth would have so many applications for my life, I hardly know where to begin. It would mean that I had better preach in a way that is faithful to the Word, and that my sermons must be able to withstand the scrutiny of people who rightly receive my preaching with eager hearts and graciously evaluate what I say against what God says in His Word.

Step five: *Shine light on the pews.* Then the Holy Spirit, through the preacher, applies the truth to the hearers, showing them what it means today. Given that I am "preaching" in this book to pastoral search committees, the timeless truth should be applied to your quest for the right kind of pastor. Here is an application appropriate for you: God will be pleased with your pastoral search committee if you make it your goal to call a pastor who will preach the Word, and if you work diligently to that end.

You get the idea. This is the call of the preacher. He must first mine the passage for truth. Then, when he understands that truth, he should apply it to his own life, and then to the lives of his listeners. When this is done, people will not go home and say something like, "Well, our pastor is kind of hung up on that." Instead, they will be faced with what God has to say. If they disagree, then they disagree with God, not with the flimsy thinking of a human being.

You Won't Be Bored

Maybe at this point you say something like, "I know we need someone who will preach the Word. But to be honest, I'm really concerned that he isn't boring." If those thoughts come to your mind, then you are not alone. This is an overriding concern for many search committees.

Let me respond to those concerns with two points. First, you cannot make it your central goal to call a pastor who will not bore you. The people in your community are drowning. They don't need someone to row out beside them and entertain them. They need the life preserver of God's Word. The people in your pews face great trials today and will in the days to come. Their most desperate need in life, even more important than whether or not they have a warm bed and food, is to hear from God. Whatever you do as a search committee, you must call a pastor who will preach the Word.

Second, if you do call a pastor who preaches the Word in a *biblical* way, then *you will not be bored*. People may get upset. A few may use the sermon time to catch up on their sleep. But if you call a truly Word-centered pastor, you can expect your church family as a whole to look forward to a weekly event where the Word is exposited and lives are changed.

What Is Not Expository Preaching

You may be better positioned to identify expository preaching if I give you an example of what expository preaching is not. Consider this outline.

Title: The Miracle of Moms

Introduction: We should all thank God for mothers. (Have mothers stand.)

1. Babies are gifts from God (Psalm 127).
   a. Tell the story of Hannah (1 Samuel 1–2).
   b. Jesus had a mother (see Gospels).
2. Being a mother is hard work (Proverbs 31:10–31).
   a. Tell stories about why being a mother is hard work. Include an incident of a child having a fever and the mother making soup.
   b. We should all work as unto the Lord (Colossians 3:22–24).
3. The Bible commands us to honor mothers (Exodus 20:3–17).
   a. Comment on the Ten Commandments being displayed in courthouses.
   b. Review the commandments.
   c. Talk about honoring mothers. Tell a story about a son who honored his mother and later became a missionary to Africa.

Conclude by telling another mother story, preferably one where the mother dies but only after giving parting instructions to her children.

Obviously, there are many biblical points in this sermon. It will connect on some levels because it speaks of one of the most glorious facets of God's plan, the gift of motherhood. But this is not expository preaching. First, it does not speak out of the authority of the Bible. Instead, it strings a series of texts together and uses them as a platform to tell emotional stories. Second, the authority of this sermon will flow not out of the text, but rather out of the emotional effect of the stories. Third, a sermon such as this will not remind people to center on Christ and His gospel. Instead, it may just encourage people to be sentimental.

A sermon is not expository simply because the preacher references Scripture. Rather, expository sermons show how the truth of God's Word nourishes the life of the listeners by helping God's people see the clear implications of the timeless meaning of Scripture for the contemporary situation.

The Summary Word

Expository preaching takes place when the truth is proclaimed and brought to bear on life. This philosophy of preaching best ensures that God's Word will be proclaimed. As for the concerns that a preacher committed to rightly expositing God's Word might prove to be boring, nothing could be further from the truth. When God's Word is rightly preached and rightly applied, it will be anything but dull. You will see God changing lives.

Before we go to the next chapter, let's review the five steps of expository preaching. If you studied it for only ten minutes, I believe you could reproduce on paper the simple box diagram shown in Chart 2. You wouldn't need to fill all the paragraphs in. Concentrate on getting the key points into the blank boxes (the diagram on the next page shows only the main headings).

Chart 3

Five Steps of Preparing an Expository Sermon

(with headings only)

Notes

1. Haddon Robinson, "The Relevance of Expository Preaching," in *Preaching to a Shifting Culture*, ed. Scott M. Gibson (Grand Rapids: Baker, 2004), 83.
2. Haddon Robinson, *Biblical Preaching*, 2nd ed. (Grand Rapids: Baker, 2001), 21.
3. If you have any question that this is the case, review the summary statements that Luke uses throughout the book that talk about how the Word of God increases and multiplies. See Acts 6:7, 9:31, 12:24, 16:5, 19:20, and 28:30–31.

CHOOSE THE MOST ABLE, holy teacher that you can have, and be not indifferent whom you hear.

Richard Baxter
The Practical Works of Richard Baxter

EVERYBODY THINKS HIMSELF a judge of a sermon, but nine out of ten might as well pretend to weigh the moon.

Charles Spurgeon
Spurgeon's Practical Wisdom

HE MUST HOLD FIRM to the trustworthy word as taught, so that he may be able to give instruction in sound doctrine and also to rebuke those who contradict it.

Titus 1:9

7

Watch More Than Just the Splash (I)

I appreciate Olympic diving. While I am not a diving expert, there are few Summer Olympic Games where I have not watched at least a portion of the diving competition. As a family, we often watch together and cheer on certain divers. My lack of technical expertise doesn't stop me from enjoying the competition.

However, consider a different scenario. What if I were given an invitation to be an actual Olympic diving judge? Let me tell you, that would be a recipe for international chaos. I would probably evaluate a Russian diver unfairly and restart the Cold War. Why? I am not equipped. It takes far more expertise to *evaluate* and judge diving than it does simply to appreciate the athleticism. About the only thing I really know is to watch the splash at the end. Less splash is better! But that would not be enough to evaluate Olympic diving justly. Being unequipped to judge divers upon absolute criteria for diving excellence, I would have to fall upon my own subjective preferences.

Similarly, if you are serving on a search committee, you have probably appreciated and benefited from preaching for many years. However, you must understand that you are about to move from being an appreciative person in the pew each week to the role of sitting in a judge's chair. Evaluating sermons requires a much deeper understanding of preaching. Many search committees are not equipped in this way; and, as a result, they do not accomplish their goal of calling an effective preacher. They evaluate preaching based only upon their subjective preferences—how much of a "splash" they see.

So how can you, as non-preachers, go about evaluating justly and wisely a candidate's preaching? The last chapter defined expository preaching by describing the process used to prepare an expository message.

The "Five Steps" chart is important. But if you are going to evaluate sermons, you will need more than this diagram. Most of the time when you evaluate a potential pastor, you will have only the outcome of the fifth box to go by: "Shine light on the pews." Unless you have a lot of time, and a very understanding candidate, you will not be able to go into his study and home and shadow him throughout the entire process of his sermon preparation. You will be able to ask specific candidates some specific questions about their preparation. But you will not do that until your committee has first homed in on a manageable number of candidates. For that reason, it is important that you be able to take only the final sermon and consider whether it is a meal of God's Word "done just right."

To help your committee evaluate the Word-centeredness of a sermon in a Word-centered way, in this chapter we will consider how to tell whether a particular sermon is truly expository.

This chapter also will help your search committee agree on the grid to follow in evaluating sermons. Without a framework for evaluating sermons, search committees typically gravitate toward subjective hunches, personal preferences, and how professionally the candidate interviews.

When Chairman Joe asked his PSC members to give their responses to the candidate's message, two had fairly subjective responses, and a third was uncomfortable giving an opinion:

Sally: "I really, really loved it. I just felt the Holy Spirit impress on my heart that this candidate is The One!"

Steve: "You know; it was okay. But I had some questions. I mean, I can't put my finger on it, but I was uncomfortable."

Chairman Joe: "Marsha, you are always the quiet one. You haven't said anything. What do you think?"

Marsha: "Well, you know, I'm on this committee mostly because of my leadership in children's ministries. I'm not sure that I am really qualified to comment on a sermon."

You can imagine where this kind of discussion leads eventually. There are different opinions and no agreed-upon criteria. Much of the dialogue is subjective, merely a summing up of how people are feeling at a given moment. Subjectivity leads either to a poor decision or no decision at all! You have probably attended enough meetings to know that an opinion-based discussion will slide in the direction of the heavyweight personalities, and if those strong personalities' opinions clash—the discussion will lead to a stalemate. Steve may ultimately defer to the opinions of the others. But what if he really was on to something with his concerns? Do we really want Marsha to remain silent? Some of the most gifted, faithful, biblically minded people in our churches work in children's ministries. Marsha may be the best evaluator in the room!

This dangerous tendency toward subjective decision-making is why it is imperative to have a reliable, predetermined set of sermon-evaluating standards that will allow you to focus on what is important and get beyond personal preferences. In this and the following two chapters, I will lay out such a grid for evaluating sermons.

Did the Sermon Preach a *Bullet*?

So what factors should you consider in sermon evaluation? Let me begin with a question that should be asked of every sermon. Was there a clear central thought for the sermon? Or put another way, did the sermon have a discernible focus? The importance of a clearly stated central thought may not be immediately apparent. I want to convince you that every sermon should be focused on a clearly stated central idea.

When a sermon is not focused on a central thought, it is impossible to follow. Imagine listening to a sermon that went something like this:

> God is a wonderful God. He has created the entire world. The mountains are so beautiful. When one looks at the mountains, he or she can feel God's presence. God's presence helps us through tough times. When I flew over Switzerland, I looked down and saw the Alps. The Alps were awesome. The trees were beautiful. Swiss people are great. God created all the people in the world. Hard times come to us all. I remember when my grandmother died. God is good.[1]

If you do not have a headache after reading that paragraph, you should. The problem is not that any one sentence is wrong or untrue. It is just that it is "scattered." The paragraph lacks focus. It is all over the place.

Saying that a sermon should have a clear central thought does *not* mean that a sermon ought to have only one point. It *does* mean that a sermon should be organized around one central concept. Haddon Robinson calls this the "big idea" of sermons. Sometimes it is called the "preaching point." Using Haddon Robinson's words, a sermon should "Fire a bullet, not buckshot."[2]

Endorsements for Firing "The Bullet"

When I first began studying preaching, I agreed with this point, but did not feel too strongly about it. However, the more I preach, the more crucial I know "firing bullets" to be. And, if you will not take my word for it, virtually every book on preaching says that a good sermon should have a clearly stated central thought or proposition. Take a few moments to read some of these other quotations. The sheer number of them that I could include testifies to the vast consensus that every sermon should be developed around a clearly stated central thought.

Haddon Robinson:

> Rhetoricians emphasize the necessity of a clearly stated central thought so strongly that virtually every textbook devotes some space to a treatment of the principle. Terminology may vary—central idea, proposition, theme, thesis statement, main thought—but the concept is the same . . . A sermon should be a bullet, not buckshot. Ideally each sermon is the explanation, interpretation, or application of a single dominant idea supported by other ideas, all drawn from one passage or several passages of Scripture.[3]

J. H. Jowett:

> I have a conviction that no sermon is ready for preaching, not ready for writing out, until we can express its theme in a short, pregnant sentence as clear as crystal. I find the getting of that sentence is the hardest, the most exacting, and the most fruitful labour in my study. To compel oneself to fashion that sentence, to dismiss every word that is vague, ragged, ambiguous, to think oneself through to a form of words which defines the theme with scrupulous exactness—this is surely one of the most vital and essential factors in the making of a sermon: and I do not think any sermon ought to be

> preached or even written, until that sentence has emerged, clear and lucid as a cloudless moon.[4]

John MacArthur:

> Make sure that every expository message has a single theme that is crystal clear so that your people know exactly what you are saying, how you have supported it, and how it is applied to their lives. The thing that kills people in what is sometimes called expository preaching is randomly meandering through a passage.[5]

Andy Stanley:

> The approach we are developing throughout this book assumes that a communicator has a destination in mind; a single idea they want to communicate; a specific thing he or she hopes to accomplish. And once that point, that idea, that destination is clear, then the goal is to bend everything in the message towards that one thing.[6]

Samuel T. Logan:

> But a sermon to be great, to be effective, whether it is long or short, must be *focused*. . . . The aim must be precise, and good preachers recognize this, often instinctively.[7]

Robert Lewis Dabney:

> Affirmatively, rhetorical unity requires these two things. The speaker must, first, have one main subject of discourse, to which he adheres with supreme reference throughout. But this is not enough. He must, second, propose to himself one definite impression on the

> hearer's soul, to the making of which everything in the sermon is bent.[8]

Fred Craddock:

> The fruit of interpretation . . . is the statement of the message in a simple affirmative sentence. That one is able to do this is the clearest evidence of the adequacy of that study which, in turn, gives permission to proceed to attending to the sermon itself.[9]

Bryan Chapell's "3 a.m. test" is especially vivid:

> The 3 a.m. test requires you to imagine [someone] awaking you from your deepest slumber with this simple question, "What's the sermon about today, Pastor?" If you cannot give a crisp answer, you know the sermon is probably half-baked. Thoughts you cannot gather at 3 a.m. are not likely to be caught by others at 11 a.m.[10]

In order to evaluate a sermon for the central thought, you need to listen to the sermon as a whole. It is possible that a sermon may have one or two powerful anecdotes that capture your imagination, hold your attention, or make you smile or cry. But do these points fit with the overall thrust of the sermon? Do they fit with the preaching point that flows out of the Bible? A preacher who makes his own points will soon wear thin. He will lack the freshness of the Spirit and the authority of the Word.

Did the Sermon Preach a *Biblical* Bullet?

The second criterion is even more important than the first. When evaluating a sermon, we must ask, "Is it true to the Bible?" If the sermon is going to be "expository," the clearly stated central thought must flow out of the Bible. Most often, this will be from one Bible passage. As you listen to the sermon and identify the central thought and points of the sermon, ask, "Is this the point of the text? Does the central thought originate from what the Bible says?"

Evaluating sermons may require that you study a particular text yourselves as committee members. Preachers often read their meanings *into* passages, rather than allowing the text to speak. Ask yourself at this point, "Did the candidate dig out the timeless truth of this passage and apply it to our situation today?" A Bible passage does not have many different "optional" meanings. It should have *one* meaning with perhaps many applications. Did the preacher speak out of the truth of the Word? This is where you get to be like the Bereans. Remember them? They were ready to examine the Word to see if what Paul said was true (Acts 17:11).

It should be pointed out that, if a sermon is true to the text, then it will ultimately be Christ-centered. Our faith is not essentially about the words of a book, and certainly not about a set of propositions. We are all about a person: the Lord Jesus Christ. His person and His redemptive work are the central theme of Scripture. Truly biblical preaching will keep us centered on Him.

Further, sermons that are true to the text are authoritative. They clearly and confidently give direction for life. But such confidence comes only if the preaching clearly flows out of the Word of God. Seminary president and expositor Albert Mohler writes:

> In all true expository preaching, there is the note of authority. That is because the preacher dares to speak on behalf of God. He stands in the pulpit as a steward "of the mysteries of God" (1 Corinthians 4:1), declaring the truth of God's Word, proclaiming the power of that Word, and applying that Word to life. This is an admittedly audacious act. No one should even contemplate such an endeavor without absolute confidence in a divine call to preach, and in the unblemished authority of the Scriptures.[11]

We can combine the first two criteria together in this sentence: *"A sermon should preach a biblical bullet."* It should be a "bullet" in that it is organized around a pointed, clearly stated central thought. A sermon should be biblical in that it faithfully reflects and flows out of the authority of Scripture.

The Summary Word

If you are going to judge Olympic diving, then you need to watch more than just the splash. If you are going to evaluate preaching, then you need to know how to look for the key components of biblical preaching. The first components are that a sermon should contain a bullet and that bullet should be "biblical"—a focused truth that flows directly out of the Word of God.

The first time I read that a sermon should be a "biblical bullet" was when I was in seminary and I was reading Haddon Robinson's book *Biblical Preaching*. As I mentioned before, I didn't disagree that a sermon should be a "biblical bullet." But I didn't view it as an especially profound point. I probably yawned even as I read it. But the more sermons I prepare, the more I study preaching, the more I actually preach—the more I understand how foundational it is for a sermon to preach a biblical bullet.

Preaching that will please the Lord and be used for eternity in the life of the church should be characterized as a biblical bullet. I will explain more in the next chapter about why biblical preaching is so powerful.

Notes

1. I am grateful to Tom Anderst and Marvin Harris for this example. They used it as an example of an unfocused paragraph.
2. Haddon Robinson, *Biblical Preaching*, 2nd ed. (Grand Rapids: Baker, 2001), 35.
3. Ibid., 35–36, 35.
4. J. H. Jowett, quoted in Robinson, *Biblical Preaching*, 37.
5. John MacArthur, "Frequently Asked Questions About Expository Preaching," in *Rediscovering Expository Preaching*, ed. Richard Mayhue (Dallas: Word, 1992), 347.
6. Andy Stanley and Lane Jones, *Communicating for a Change* (Sisters, Oreg.: Multnomah, 2006), 101.
7. Samuel T. Logan, "The Phenomenology of Preaching," in *The Preacher and Preaching*, ed. Samuel T. Logan (Phillipsburg, N.J.: Presbyterian and Reformed, 1986), 129.
8. Robert Lewis Dabney, *Sacred Rhetoric* (Richmond, Va.: Presbyterian, 1870), 109.
9. Fred Craddock, *Preaching* (Nashville: Abingdon, 1985), 155.
10. Bryan Chapell, *Christ-Centered Preaching* (Grand Rapids: Baker, 1994), 39.
11. R. Albert Mohler, *He Is Not Silent* (Chicago: Moody, 2008), 71.

What is preaching? Logic on fire! Eloquent reason! Are these contradictions? Of course they are not. Reason concerning this Truth ought to be mightily eloquent, as you see it in the case of the Apostle Paul and others. It is theology on fire. And a theology which does not take fire, I maintain, is a defective theology.

David Martyn Lloyd-Jones
Preaching and Preachers

What did Wesley have that made his sermons so powerful? The answer is *nothing*. It was not the man who made the message move people with such power.

Will Willimon
Proclamation and Theology

And [pray] also for me, that words may be given to me in opening my mouth boldly to proclaim the mystery of the gospel, for which I am an ambassador in chains, that I may declare it boldly, as I ought to speak.

Ephesians 6:19–20

8

Watch More Than Just the Splash (II)

I think it would be cool to have a time machine—just dial in a particular date and visit an historical event. Biblical events aside, one of my first stops would be the First Great Awakening, a revival that started around 1740 and took place predominantly in England and North America. As is the case in all great revivals, the principal means God used to bring about that revival was the preaching of the Word. Some of the greatest preachers ever, including George Whitefield and Jonathan Edwards, preached during this great revival.

Of course, I don't have access to a time machine, so I content myself to reading eyewitness accounts. This testimony of a farmer named Nathan Coles describes how God stirred people to hear the Word preached and to respond to Whitefield's preaching early in the First Great Awakening. See if you can picture in your mind this farmer, out working in his fields when he heard that Whitefield was scheduled to preach nearby.

> Now it pleased God to send Mr. Whitefield into this land and my hearing of his preaching at Philadelphia, like one of the old apostles, and many thousands flocking after him to hear the gospel and great numbers converted to Christ, I felt the Spirit of God drawing me by conviction. . . . Next I heard he was on Long Island and next at Boston and next at Northampton and then, one morning, all on a sudden, about 8 or 9 o'clock there came a messenger and said, "Mr. Whitefield preached at Hartford and Wethersfield yesterday and is to preach at Middletown this morning at 10 o'clock."
>
> I was in my field, at work. I dropped my tool that I had in my hand, ran home and ran through my house and bade my wife get ready quick to go and hear Mr. Whitefield preach at Middletown and ran to my pasture for my horse with all my might, fearing I should be too late to hear him. I brought my horse home and soon mounted and took my wife up and went forward as fast as she could and not stop or slack for me except I bade her, and so I would run until I was almost out of breath and then mount my horse again, and so I did several times to favour my

> horse . . . for we had twelve miles to ride double in little more than an hour. . . .
>
> When we got down to the old meeting house there was a great multitude—it was said to be 3 or 4000 people assembled together. We got off from our [horse] and shook off the dust, and the ministers were then coming to the meetinghouse. I turned and looked towards the great river and saw ferry boats running swift, forward and backward, bringing over loads of people, the oars rowed nimble and quick. Everything, men, horses and boats, all seemed to be struggling for life; the land and the banks over the river looked black with people and horses. All along the 12 miles, I saw no man at work in his field, but all seemed to be gone.[1]

The last chapter stressed that a sermon should be a "biblical bullet." The words "biblical" and "bullet" are both important. A sermon should be a "bullet" in that it should be singly focused. And, above all, the central thought or bullet must be *true to the biblical text.* It must flow *out of* the truth of Scripture.

As important and foundational as these two points are, if we were to stop with them, then preaching could be nothing more than an academic exercise that consisted of identifying a biblical truth and delivering it pointedly. The mere emission of "biblical bullets" could not account for the spectacular ways crowds gathered and then responded to the preaching of God's Word during the Great Awakening and other times of revival. What is it about the preaching of the Word that God uses supernaturally to cut hearts asunder? The next characteristic of expository preaching speaks to that question.

Did the Sermon *Fire* a Biblical Bullet?

Biblical preaching should be *fired*! That is, preachers should proclaim the Word with a special *unction,* or Spirit-empowered boldness. The word "unction" may not be familiar to you. Where preaching is concerned, it refers to "a Spirit-empowered boldness that enables us to proclaim the gospel with boldness, clarity and power."[2] Lee Eclov summarizes it this way: "*Unction* means the anointing of the Holy Spirit on a sermon so that something holy and powerful is added to the message that no preacher can generate, no matter how great his skills."[3]

Unction was Paul's goal when he preached. In giving prayer requests to the Ephesians, he asked for prayer in the following way: "And also for me, that words may be given to me in opening my mouth *boldly* to proclaim the mystery of the gospel, for which I am an ambassador in chains, that I may declare it *boldly,* as I ought to speak" (Ephesians 6:19–20, emphasis added).

When Paul asks for prayer that he would be "bold," he isn't talking about merely the absence of fear. We know from elsewhere in Scripture that there were times when he felt fear, but knew his preaching to be effectual in spite of his fear. He wrote to the Corinthians:

> *And I, when I came to you, brothers, did not come proclaiming to you the testimony of God with lofty*

speech or wisdom. For I decided to know nothing among you except Jesus Christ *and him crucified. And I was with you in weakness and in fear and much trembling, and my speech and my message were not in plausible words of wisdom, but in demonstration of the Spirit and of power, that your faith might not rest in the wisdom of men but in the power of God.*
(1 Corinthians 2:1–5)

Basically, Paul is saying, "I was scared. But *it didn't matter* that I had weakness and fear and trembling." Nor was it of concern to Paul that his words weren't particularly brilliant in terms of a human assessment. Paul's preaching was life-changing in spite of his fear, in spite of his other limitations—*because* he had been given *unction*: A Spirit-given boldness that wielded the Word with power to change the lives of receptive listeners. This Spirit-empowered unction allowed Paul to preach the Word not only boldly, but also understandably and clearly.

A great example of preaching with unction is found in Acts 4. Here the Greek word for "boldness" that Paul used in Ephesians 6:19–20 appears twice. Peter and John pray for *unction*—or, as it is translated here—"boldness."

"And now, Lord, look upon their threats and grant to your servants to continue to speak your word with all boldness, *while you stretch out your hand to heal, and signs and wonders are performed through the name of your holy servant Jesus." And when they had prayed, the place in which they were gathered together was*

> *shaken, and they were all filled with the Holy Spirit and continued to speak the word of God with* boldness. (Acts 4:29–31, emphasis added)

Whatever the listeners were feeling during the preaching in Acts 4, you would not have heard any of them grumbling about "boredom" or complaining that the sermon seemed "irrelevant." Working powerfully in their midst, the Holy Spirit gave remarkable unity and grace (Acts 4:32, *ff.*).

Returning to Paul's prayer request to the Ephesians: He requested prayer support that he would have this unction, this Spirit-empowered boldness, so that he could make known the mystery of the gospel. The gospel is a "mystery" in the sense that it can be understood only through the work of the Holy Spirit in conjunction with His Word. In Christ, the full plan of salvation can be clearly understood. Paul points to this in First Corinthians:

> *Now we have received not the spirit of the world, but the Spirit who is from God, that we might understand the things freely given us by God. And we impart this in words not taught by human wisdom but taught by the Spirit, interpreting spiritual truths to those who are spiritual. The natural person does not accept the things of the Spirit of God, for they are folly to him, and he is not able to understand them because they are spiritually discerned.* (1 Corinthians 2:12–14)

Both the Bible and the history of human civilization describe many examples of powerful responses when God's

Word is preached. In Acts 4, when the Word is preached with such evidently Spirit-given *unction*, we read, "Great grace was upon them all" (Acts 4:33). The last word in Acts about the apostle Paul was that he continued preaching the Word with all boldness. Again we could substitute the word "unction" in place of this idea of Spirit-empowered "boldness." In a sense, Luke doesn't end the book of Acts. He wants the reader to know that the story of the spread of the Word through preaching is *still* being written.

Cautions about Bullet-Firings

A couple of words of caution are in order here: When evaluating whether a sermon was "fired," the question ought not be, "Did a great *revival* take place?" Nor should the question be, "Did that sermon reap the kind of responses that Whitefield and Edwards saw?" Times of revival like the Great Awakening are rare. Rather, the question you as a pastoral search committee ought to be asking is this: "Did this candidate's preaching evidence a spiritual boldness and clarity that demonstrates his reliance on the Holy Spirit and his conviction that God's Word is powerful and useful?"

Secondly, when I say that a sermon should be a "biblical bullet *fired*" at the life of the listener, I do not mean to imply anything significant about the sermon's length, its emotional pull, or its employment of humorous anecdotes. The extent to which any preacher uses any of these stylistic elements will vary a great deal. Surely, there are great preachers who include humor in their sermons. Spurgeon, the "Prince of Preachers," used humor freely in his sermons, but it never minimized the spiritual urgency nor the sober applications of his sermons. Others—like Whitefield—spoke with great eloquence and drama, whereas Jonathan Edwards was far less outwardly demonstrative—yet the Holy Spirit used the preaching of these men to effect absolutely sensational spiritual results.[4]

The point of asking if a sermon is "fired," asking if it truly has *unction*, is to consider whether or not it exhibits a Spirit-empowered boldness and clarity.

The Summary Word

This chapter argues that a sermon should be *"a biblical bullet fired."* This is one of the first three criteria for evaluating a sermon:

1. A sermon should have a clear central thought or focus; that is, contain a bullet.
2. The central thought of a sermon should flow out of the authoritative Word of God; that is, contain a *biblical* bullet.
3. The sermon should be preached with unction or Spirit-empowered boldness and clarity; that is, this biblical bullet should be "fired."

These three criteria offer a sure foundation for evaluating preaching. But, in order to be effective, a bullet that is fired must also be aimed in a very careful way. We will be talking about a kind of biblical marksmanship in the next chapter.

NOTES

1. Excerpt taken from Nathan Coles' manuscript "Spiritual Travels," part of which is printed in G. L. Walker, *Some Aspects of the Religious Life of New England,* (n.p., 1897), 89–91; as quoted in Ian H. Murray, *Jonathan Edwards: A New Biography* (Carlisle, Pa.: The Banner of Truth, 1996), 164.
2. John H. Armstrong, *True Revival* (Eugene, Oreg.: Harvest House, 2001), 139.
3. Lee Eclov, "How Does Unction Function?" in *The Art and Craft of Biblical Preaching,* ed. Haddon Robinson and Craig Brian Larson (Grand Rapids: Zondervan, 2005), 81.
4. George M. Marsden, *Jonathan Edwards* (New Haven & London: Yale Univ. Press, 2003), 206.

AUTHENTIC CHRISTIAN PREACHING is *both biblical and contemporary.* It is an exposition of Scripture which is related to the world in which we live.

John Stott
The Living Church

THEY WANTED TO KNOW the truth because they loved the truth. So they checked to make sure that what the apostle Paul was saying matched up with the truth of God's Word. If the Bereans were screening the apostle Paul, who was speaking under the direct inspiration of the Holy Spirit, how much more should you screen what you hear in church.

Ken Ramey
Expository Listening

ALL SCRIPTURE IS BREATHED out by God and *profitable* for teaching, for reproof, for correction, and for training in righteousness.

2 Timothy 3:16 (italics added)

9

Watch More Than Just the Splash (III)

So far, we've considered three criteria that should be used to evaluate preaching: a *bullet* (central thought) that is *biblical* is *fired* with unction (Spirit-empowered boldness). Putting these three criteria together, we have a good start on how to evaluate candidates' sermons rightly: *"A sermon should fire a biblical bullet."*

But this start begs a crucial question—If a sermon is a biblical bullet, *where should it be aimed*?

Did the Sermon Fire a Biblical Bullet Aimed *at the Life of the Listener*?

A sermon should be both true to the text, and it should be "true to the audience." An effective pastor will preach with the key sermon point aimed right at the listener.

When I teach about preaching, I will often work through this straightforward exercise. First, I ask someone to read Titus 2:1: "But as for you, teach what accords with sound doctrine."

I then ask, "What does Paul tell Titus to teach or preach?" Usually, someone quickly responds with great conviction, "sound doctrine." I then smile and say back to them, "Wrong!" Paul does not say to teach sound doctrine. Rather, Paul says, "teach *what accords with* sound doctrine."

This is no minor detail. The word "accords" is very important. Paul does not tell Titus simply to preach "sound doctrine." He says to preach that which "fits" or "is appropriate" or "accords" with sound doctrine. The Greek word here means "to be fitting, be seemly or suitable." Paul is exhorting Titus to show how sound doctrine fits with life. The pastor you are seeking should preach a message that meets the daily needs of the listener. Just as our culture and fashion inform and form our understanding of what is appropriate to wear to a formal function, preachers should show their people the kind of behavior that ought to adorn their lives.

It is through expository preaching that the Word of God is heard and that "life is thought about and given its most searching and serious analysis."[1] Haddon Robinson states, "The purpose behind each individual sermon is to secure some moral action."[2] Another author, Joe Stowell, writes, "But if ultimately the outcome does not result in a changed life because of an encounter with truth, then it has not been what God intended preaching to be."[3] And along the same lines—the intersection between theological truth and everyday life application—this is what Duane Litfin has to say: "The purpose of Scripture is not merely to satisfy our curiosity or to provide us with a glimpse of something that happened long ago. It is designed to transform lives today, and the expositor acknowledges this by always helping the audience to come to grips with the relevance of the passage for them."[4]

After Paul reminded Timothy that all Scripture is "God-breathed" (2 Timothy 3:16 NIV), he told Timothy to preach the Word (4:1–2), insisting that Scripture is "useful." The Bible is not boring, because it is useful for something. Paul tells Timothy that Scripture contributes "teaching, rebuking, correcting and training in righteousness" (3:16b). Scripture is relevant for life, and the sermon should apply it to the listeners' lives.

As you listen to a candidate's sermon, you must remember that it is not enough for the sermon merely to *contain* truth. Ask yourself whether the truth is being *applied to* the life of the listener. Listen throughout the sermon for points that are stated in terms of actions and exhortations. Watch for clues that the preacher is tuned into the lives of his listeners (at least as much as possible given the extent to which he's been able to get to know them as yet). Also, notice whether the preacher seems to have been impacted personally. Preaching that is true to the audience should begin with the preacher. The Word should first impact his life.

So, to sum up the criteria so far: "A sermon should be a biblical bullet fired at the life of the listener."

Did the Sermon *Clearly* Fire a Biblical Bullet At the Life of the Listener?

Preaching a sermon is like being the lead car of a caravan on a journey. The preacher must look often in his rearview mirror to make sure that listeners are not losing their way in a traffic jam of sentences or a fog of vague ideas. Listeners should be able to follow the preacher from one point to the next point. With sermon points that turn too abruptly or that reach too widely, a preacher will shake off some of the listeners from the tail end of the caravan.

As a committee, you should not excuse a sermon's lack of clarity on the assumption that vague content must indicate really "deep" content. Robinson notes, "Sometimes what we call 'deep' is simply muddy."[5] Spurgeon makes the guilty cringe when he charges:

> An average hearer, who is unable to follow the course of thought of the preacher, ought not to worry himself, but to blame the preacher, whose business it is to make the matter plain. If you look down into a well, if it be empty it will appear to be very deep, but if there be water in it you will see its brightness. I believe that many "deep" preachers are simply so because they are like dry wells with nothing whatever in them, except decaying leaves, a few stones, and perhaps a dead cat or two. If there be living water in your preaching it may be very deep, but the light of truth will give clearness to it. It is not enough to be so plain that you can be understood; you must speak so that you cannot be misunderstood.[6]

When you evaluate a sermon, ask, "Is it clear? Can I follow the progression? Do I know how he moved from one point to the next? Does it fit together?" A *clear* sermon is marked by several characteristics. These include:

- *Understandable language.* It is one thing for a preacher to introduce important theological terms like *justification* or even *propitiation*, especially if he introduces these needful concepts with straightforward, understandable definitions and explanations. But the clarity of his message will diminish if he insists on only heady vocabulary.

- *Use of restatement often.* Restatement is saying the same thing in different words. This must be done with some delicacy—restatement is *not* simply a matter of repeating the same few phrases over and over again, redundantly, over and over again, ad nauseam, etc. When evaluating a sermon, listen to see if the preacher is taking the time to restate major points.

- *The right use of illustrations.* Do the illustrations help teach the point of the text? Or are they just entertaining stories? Are there illustrations present?

- *Clear transitions to new points.* When preachers move from one point to the next without any segues to help listeners "connect the dots," they might as well be tossing clarity out the window.

The life-and-death importance of preaching demands that sermons be clear. "When people leave a church in a mental fog, they do so at their spiritual peril."[7] For the love of God and for the love of His people, you *must* ask yourselves, "Was this sermon clear?"

Summarizing the criteria thus far: A sermon should clearly fire a biblical bullet at the life of the listener.

Was the Sermon *Interesting*?

What is implicit in the above question is that good preaching should also be *interesting*. There is no doubt that some preaching is terribly boring. That is not okay!

Spurgeon was ruthless in his criticisms of boring preaching. Here is how he described boring sermons: "No [*anesthetic*] can ever equal some discourses in sleep-giving properties; no human being, unless gifted with infinite patience, could long endure to listen to them, and nature does well to give the victim deliverance through sleep."

As for the preachers, he said: "If some men were sentenced to hear their own sermons it would be a righteous judgment upon them, and they would soon cry out with Cain, 'My punishment is far greater than I can bear.'" [8]

We could debate whether boring preachers deserve such dire punishment. But your church does not want to call a preacher who will put you to sleep for years to come. As you evaluate sermons, you should also consider whether or not the preacher holds your interest. Do his illustrations seem canned or trite? Do the illustrations draw you in? Is the sermon too predictable? Does the preacher seem to sense when he is losing people's attention? Does he seem to be able to make adjustments accordingly? Do you find yourself wondering how the sermon will end, or wondering *if it ever will end*?

Did the Sermon Have Effective Gestures and Nonverbal Communication?

Here are some additional criteria to evaluate the sermon, expressed as one question: "How were the gestures, nonverbal communication, and overall presentation?" The preacher's movements should seem natural, and his body language should reinforce the message and seem appropriate. His movements should not draw attention to himself nor be distracting.

Going Beyond the Splash: An Evaluation Form

We have looked in chapters 7–9 at many criteria for evaluating a prospective pastor's preaching. To pull it all together, this chapter ends with an evaluation form that summarizes all of the criteria. At the very end I suggest a "weighted" system for scoring the sermon. I admit right up front that I have a background in science.

You may say, "Well, this is way too technical, too complicated." Honestly, it isn't that bad. The weighted scoring system is just a way of showing that some parts of the sermon evaluation are indeed more important than others. The suggested scoring system would put the most emphasis on the more crucial expectations of a biblical "bullet" being clearly fired at the life of the listener.

I would suggest that, for each sermon, each committee member should fill out and submit a form for *all* committee members to review *before* discussing that particular sermon. This group-wide access to the evaluation forms will protect the committee from losing the valuable insights of less vocal participants who might otherwise hesitate to share their evaluations in a group discussion.

Some Final Suggestions

Here are a few more suggestions for evaluating sermons.

First, consider selecting sermon recordings to listen to randomly, *and* letting the candidate suggest some selections. For example, you might say to the candidate, "Please send us the last four sermons you preached." But you might be wise to add this request: "Please also send us a couple sermons of your own choosing." It can be nice to know what *he* thinks is one of his better efforts.

Second, encourage one another to listen to sermons at a time when you can give them your undivided attention. This may not be possible for all sermons, but do so whenever possible, and especially as you zero in on a few candidates.

Third, be open to giving a preacher less-than-perfect scores. In researching this book, I found that people on pastoral search committees do hesitate to be critical. Don't forget the exhortation of Part 2: "Judge, *lest you be judged*." While preachers, myself included, do appreciate people who are gracious in their evaluation, careful discrimination in choosing a candidate is necessary because so much is at stake.

When you evaluate a sermon, keep the following in mind:

- Maintain an attitude of humility and grace. Preaching is so challenging. Approach your evaluation as though you were going to present it to the preacher being evaluated and his family.

- At the same time, only Jesus preached perfect sermons. You will not hear a perfect sermon. Do not feel as though you are being mean or wrongly judgmental if you note how a sermon might be improved.

- Be slow to score too highly too soon. This is a principle you can learn from Olympic judges. The judges will make sure when they evaluate an early candidate that they do not put the early scores up against the ceiling. Likewise, you need to make sure that if you were to hear an even stronger sermon from the same candidate that you have left yourself a little room to distinguish which sermon would receive higher scores between the two.

Sermon Evaluation Form

Preacher:	**Sermon Title:**
Date Preached:	**Date Heard:**
Start Time:	**End Time:**
Evaluator:	

For each of the following areas, score the candidate's sermon from 1 to 5 (5 being the best possible), and add comments.

Was there a clear central thought or focus for the sermon?

1 2 3 4 5

What *was* the central thought?

Was the sermon faithful to the biblical text?

1 2 3 4 5

Did the sermon show evidence of a holy *unction* (an anointing of the Holy Spirit)? Was there spiritual boldness and urgency?

1 2 3 4 5

Was the sermon aimed as accurately as possible into the hearts of the audience *where* the sermon was preached? (Don't evaluate him as though he were preaching this message to your church.)

1 2 3 4 5

Was the sermon clear and easy to follow?

1 2 3 4 5

Was the sermon interesting?

1 2 3 4 5

How were the gestures, nonverbal communication, and overall presentation?

1 2 3 4 5

Do you have any other thoughts or comments?

What two or three things were done well in the sermon that you would hope to see repeated in future sermons?

What are two or three things that might have made this sermon better?

Calculating a Final Score

"A sermon should clearly fire a biblical bullet at the life of the listener."

Category	***Initial Score***	***Weight Multiplier***	***Final Scores* (= IS x WM)***
A bullet: Was there a clear central thought or focus for the sermon?		**4**	
Biblical: Was the sermon faithful to the biblical text?		**5**	
Fired: Did the sermon show evidence of a holy unction (an anointing of the Holy Spirit)? Was there spiritual boldness and urgency?		**4**	
At the life of the listener: Was the sermon aimed as accurately as possible into the hearts of the audience where the sermon was preached?		**2**	
Clearly: Was the sermon clear and easy to follow?		**2**	
Was the sermon interesting?		**2**	
How were the gestures, nonverbal communication, and overall presentation?		**1**	
***TOTAL**			

* The "Final Scores" column's contents should be figured across each row by multiplying the "Initial Score" column contents by the "Weight Multiplier" value next to each. Then, the TOTAL box should simply be the sum of the "Final Scores" column contents. Using the weight multipliers suggested above, the highest score possible would be 100.

Notes

1. David F. Wells, *God in the Wasteland* (Grand Rapids: Eerdmans, 1994), 84. Wells says, "The church should be known as a place where God is worshiped, where the Word of God is heard and practiced, and where life is thought about and given its most searching and serious analysis."
2. Haddon Robinson, *Biblical Preaching,* 2nd ed. (Grand Rapids: Baker, 2001), 107.
3. Joseph Stowell, "Preaching for Change," in *The Big Idea of Biblical Preaching,* ed. Keith Willhite and Scott M. Gibson (Grand Rapids: Baker, 1998), 125.
4. A. Duane Litfin, *Public Speaking: A Handbook for Christians,* 2nd ed. (Grand Rapids: Baker, 1992), 340.
5. Haddon Robinson and Scott M. Gibson, *Making a Difference in Preaching* (Grand Rapids: Baker, 1999), 26.
6. C. H. Spurgeon, *Lectures to My Students: Complete & Unabridged,* new ed. (Grand Rapids: Zondervan, 1954), 210.
7. Robinson, *Biblical Preaching,* 46.
8. Spurgeon, *Lectures to My Students,* 209.

Part 3

Make Those Dates (Interviews) Count

IN THE INTRODUCTION to this book, I compared the pastoral search to the process of looking for a spouse. I pointed out that often a mutual acquaintance is the first to introduce a church to their next pastor. It all starts out casually enough, with some superficial investigation. But sooner or later, as things progress, it comes time for a "first date," or using more contextual vocabulary, an interview. If that initial meeting goes well, there may be more to come.

Here's the thing. You've got to make those "dates" count! If you are interviewing a candidate, then it means he is a serious possibility. This is your chance to collect a great deal of data that will help you make a wise decision.

To help you with the interviewing process, chapter 10 will outline interviewing principles before suggesting a number of interview questions. Chapter 11 will give insights how to interview candidates about preaching. This will be followed with final thoughts, questions and answers, and recommended reading.

A WELL-CONDUCTED INTERVIEW always focuses on getting people to elaborate in detail about their past accomplishments. Use open-ended questions to encourage a conversation, not just yes-no answers . . . The most important question to ask in an interview is the follow-up question. Don't let candidates get away with just providing their rehearsed answers to your inquiries about past accomplishments.

Eric Herrenkohl
How to Hire A-Players

THIS IS WHY I LEFT YOU in Crete, so that you might put what remained into order, and appoint elders in every town as I directed you.

Titus 1:5

10

Principles for Interviewing

Chapter 11 has more than three dozen questions for interviewing a pastoral candidate. But don't go there yet. First consider these seven basic principles to keep in mind while interviewing:

1. Don't Try to Get All the Answers in One Interview

You don't have to accomplish everything in one interview. Before you would extend an actual call to your next pastor, a great deal of interaction ought to have taken place between your church and the candidate already. Take good notes. Share them with one another. But don't feel as though you have to ask all of your questions in one single interview.

The number of interviews will vary with different churches.[1] Typically, however, there are at least three times of interviewing.

- An initial interview to evaluate if a candidate is a possible fit. This will often take place as a conference call or with the pastoral search committee visiting a candidate in his home.
- An invitation for a potential candidate to come to the church, which may or may not be over a Sunday. During this visit, several different groups may interview a candidate. This set of interviews is very important. Three or four interviews might each last one-and-one-half to two hours.
- Churches who ask a pastor to candidate may also schedule question-and-answer periods for the congregation as a whole.

2. Remember That Interviewing Is a Two-Way Street

To be sure, you are a evaluating a potential candidate. But remember that he is also evaluating your church and the prospect of a life-altering, perhaps even a lifelong, move to become a part of your church. In most cases, agreeing to become your pastor will mean that he must relocate his family and lead them in investing their lives into your church and community.

Considering the level of commitment required on his

part, and on behalf of your church, be sure to put your best foot forward. If at all possible, allow him to stay in a hotel so that he can have private time and comfortable quarters during his visit. Consider putting a basket of refreshments and a special welcome card in the room before he arrives. If the interview process continues or the visits become frequent or long, invite and accommodate his wife, as well, so that they can undergo the process together and consider the possibility together.

3. Be Ready to Ask Questions about What He's Already Done

Seek out concrete evidence from the candidate's past record to see how he might lead your church in the future. It can be easy to spend your interview time talking theoretically about what a pastor might do if he were to be called to your church. There *is* a place for talking about what he envisions for your church's future, about what he could or would do one day at your church. But while hypothesizing and dreaming can be beneficial, the better measure of your candidate's capacities would be getting a good understanding of what he has actually accomplished in the past. How has he handled difficult circumstances? How has he responded during times of trial? How has he followed through on past plans and projects? What has he already accomplished?

Don't just pose merely hypothetical interview questions. Pose behavioral questions. Ask him what he has already done, or how he now believes he should have handled a past situation differently. That will give you a more accurate reading on what he might do in the future. Tommy Thomas, a human resources consultant, explains the concept this way:

> I have been in several interviews that included questions such as: "If you were hired for this position, how would you . . . ?" or "What would you do if . . . ?" This is not the way to frame a question to get the most helpful response. Over the past forty-five years, my colleagues and I have collectively interviewed over six hundred thousand people, and we have learned that you get the most helpful data when you focus on specifics that the candidate has done in his past.
>
> Knowing what the candidate has done in the past will predict how she will perform in the future. You want to ask questions, therefore, about what she has done and how she has performed in her past positions. This is behavioral interviewing.[2]

Most of the questions listed below are worded to ask a candidate to articulate what he *has done,* rather than asking the candidate to speculate about what he *would do.* Be prepared to follow up his answers with still more probing questions that elicit the kind of answers that pull from his concrete experience rather than force him to hypothesize about abstract ideals. Probe until you are completely satisfied with an answer given by an applicant.

Questions that could help to clarify responses include:

- Why do you feel that way?
- Anything else?
- Why do you say that?
- What do you think causes that?
- If a younger leader were to find himself in a similar situation and came to you for counsel, how would you advise him?
- If you had to relive that situation, what changes would you make to the way you handled it?
- Why was that such a disappointment to you?
- Can you give me another example?[3]

4. Think toward Finding the Right "Fit" For Your Particular Church

There are many gifted, godly leaders out there. Only *one* of them is called to pastor your church. Go into your interview with a prioritized list of specific qualities that you are seeking in a pastor for your church. Your interview questions should be designed to evaluate the candidate's strengths and weaknesses in terms of those specific qualities that you have delineated as high-priority concerns for your church.

By "specific," I mean that you should be probing the candidate's capacity to adjust to particular things about your particular church. For example, if your church is located in a rural community, you would want to draw out some answers that would help you determine whether this candidate and his family would adapt well to a rural environment. That does not mean he necessarily must hail from a rural community himself. But you ought to evaluate how much of an adjustment that would require for him and his family, and you ought to seek some evidence that they would be capable of making such an adjustment.

5. Don't Confuse Good Interviewing Skills with Good Pastoring Skills

We return to human resources consultant Tommy Thomas for one caution in judging the interviewee:

> Beware of the "smile factor." This is where you have to be very careful. Competency to do a job and the ability to sell oneself are not the same thing. Unfortunately, when it comes to making hiring decisions, the individuals doing the interviewing and hiring frequently fail to make this distinction. The result? The two are often confused. The person with more polish than substance is often hired, and the selection process fails to find the best person for the job.[4]

Just because someone interviews well does not mean that he will be an effective pastor. The reality is, he might just be good at selling himself.

The converse is also true. It may be that the right man for the job, the best possible shepherd for your flock, presents himself miserably in an interview. It takes patience and wisdom, and perhaps further interviews, to get to the bottom of someone and discern whether he would be the right fit for your church.

When I was the senior pastor of a different church, a search committee and I interviewed a qualified candidate for a staff position. I had done my homework prior to bringing him to the church to interview. I was convinced that he was both qualified *and* a good fit for our church. However, during the interviews with our church family, he said several things that raised flags for some of our people. Interviewing wasn't his strong point, and his performance literally almost ended the candidating process.

Eventually, after some heart-to-heart discussions and intense prayer, we determined that his answers had not reflected weakness in his theology nor an inability to do the job. We did end up calling him as associate pastor. He has now been serving faithfully and effectually in that church for more than ten years. He was the right man for the job. It would have been a terrible mistake if we had concluded that just because he mishandled a couple of questions, he would automatically make for a poor pastor.

6. If Possible, Visit the Candidate at His Church and in His Home

For a candidate whom you are seriously investigating, if possible, arrange a personal or group trip to visit him at his own church and in his home. Interviews are about collecting as much data about a candidate as possible, and you would do well as a committee to investigate the candidate's personal life to a degree in territory that's familiar to him.

If at some point in the process, you are able to enter into a candidate's home and "comfort zones," it gives him a little bit of "home court advantage," but it also will allow you an inside opportunity to learn a great deal about him. If the candidate is able to have you visit him in his own home, then by default you will be able to evaluate his hospitality (Titus 1:8). If he has a wife and children, you may have an opportunity to see how they relate together as a family.

For this kind of in-depth interviewing "mission," your church will have to spend some money to cover travel costs of the interviewer(s). Encourage the congregation that it is worth the extra expenditure to ensure your team is able to make a quality decision.

One author summarized several advantages of observing a pastoral candidate in his own setting.

The advantages of seeing a pastor on his own home turf are:

- You see the whole person, not a truncated version. He's interacting with real people. The way he greets folks as they leave is as telling as what he does during the service.
- You can get an idea of the type of people he attracts. One of the winsome factors about our candidate was the warmth of his congregation.
- It shows the pastor that you are seriously interested. If he's a reluctant candidate, it's probably a watershed where he has to decide if he's serious about relocating or just playing games because the interest is flattering.

- The travel is a catalyst in drawing [the pastoral search committee] members together. "We were often at each other's throats until we sat together on a Sunday morning in Milwaukee eating bratwurst or got lost trying to find a church in Cleveland."[5]

7. Interview about Preaching

Be sure to cover the subject of *preaching* when you're interviewing a *preacher*! Even if you have heard him deliver one or more solid sermons, spend time questioning him *about* preaching. Many pastors would claim preaching as their number one strength. A careful interview is necessary to perceive beyond a candidate's simply *telling* you that preaching is his forte.

You might respond, "Oh, we would never overlook questions about preaching." Be careful. Time spent on good questions in other areas can easily crowd out a careful examination of the candidate's views on preaching. You will examine a potential pastor about *many* things, and these are all needful things to know. You will want to ask about his work ethic and how he relates to staff and church leaders. Is he responsible with his personal finances? Has he also shown discretion and stewardship in his past interactions with ministry finances? You will want to learn about his personality and affinities and adaptability to probe whether there could be the right chemistry between this man and your church and community. During this exchange, the candidate will probably be directing some questions back toward you.

Before you know it, your time for interview questions will be up. If it's a first interview, the conference call time may be over. If it's during a visit from a candidate, you will need to leave for a dinner reservation or a tour of the community.

Even if you have listened to a number of his actual sermons, grilling a potential pastor about preaching is critical for several reasons:

- You want to be confident that your next preaching pastor is truly committed to preaching "biblical bullets" consistently. It could be that the sermon(s) you have heard do not accurately represent what a pastor has accomplished or planned over the long haul.
- Even if you heard a good sermon from this candidate, you need to acknowledge the possibility that it might have been plagiarized, or that the sermon you heard could've been his "one-hit wonder."
- It may be that a potential candidate has not yet served in a pulpit ministry. Sermon recordings or opportunities to hear him preach in person may be limited. Further, if he has not yet been in a regular preaching ministry, then he will grow considerably in his preaching over time. You need to know whether he is currently at an acceptable level of preaching, but you also need to be able to discern whether he has the potential and commitment to develop his expository preaching over the months and years to come.

Interviewing a potential pastor about his views on preaching will require time. At the very least, your search committee should plan thirty to sixty minutes for this topic alone. Remember, you are praying that your next pastor will be preaching in your church for hours and hours, and for years and years to come. In light of the hours your congregation will spend under his preaching, the time it takes to conduct a thorough investigation into it is a relatively minuscule investment of time.

It might help to divide interview questions about preaching into two broad areas: First, "Is the candidate *committed* to biblical preaching?" Where is his heart? Second, "Can this potential pastor consistently *deliver* biblical preaching?" Does the candidate understand the process that preparing a *Word-centered* message requires, and that he ought to be living it out during sermon preparation? Chapter 11 suggests specific questions for interviewing candidates about preaching.

The Summary Word

A pastoral search is a marathon of unknown length. While long-distance runners know how far it is until they cross the finish line, church leaders don't know how many more laps they must run before a pastor is called. The unknown length of the pastoral search process, along with the normal challenges of life, often tempt pastoral search committees to be less than thorough during the interview process. But the stakes are too high to rush.

If you find yourself wanting to just get through the process and be done with it, take a few moments to review the principles from this chapter. Read through the suggested questions in the next chapter and identify any that may be appropriate for your situation. More important, pray that the Holy Spirit would give your team the wisdom and strength to interview well.

Notes

1. The number of interviews will depend on factors that vary from church to church. In my experience, it would not be unusual to have more than fifteen hours of interviews. See "Leading the Pastoral Search" under Recommended Reading, for resources that are more process-oriented.
2. Tommy W. Thomas, *The Perfect Search* (Grand Rapids: Credo House, 2009), 118.
3. These questions are not original to me. However, I am unaware of the original source.
4. Thomas, *The Perfect Search*, 114.
5. Em Griffin, "Confessions of a Pulpit Committee, *Leadership* (1983): 110.

The toughest part about visiting another church is the inner knowledge that you may soon want to steal their pastor. That induces guilt when the woman next to you in the pew welcomes you warmly as a visitor and even raves about their minister. More than once I felt like a spy whose cover was about to be blown.

Em Griffin
"Confessions of a Pulpit Committee" in *Leadership*

He lays the beams of his chambers on the waters; he makes the clouds his chariot; he rides on the wings of the wind; he makes his messengers winds, his ministers a flaming fire.

Psalm 104:3–4

11

Suggested Interview Questions

As you begin interviewing candidates, it is a good idea to agree as a pulpit search committee on a number of questions that you will ask candidates. This will help to more evenly compare candidates. It will also allow you to divide questions among pastoral search committee members to be sure that everyone is involved in the dialogue and assure other leaders that you are being thorough with the process.

My intent here is not to present either an exhaustive set of questions or a script to follow in an interview. It would be a very long interview if you tried to cover all of these at once. Rather, you can choose which questions to ask at various points throughout the process of evaluating candidates.

Questions About the Candidate's Call to Ministry and His Particular Context

1. *Ask those questions about connections.* Find out whether the candidate knows anyone whom you know. I call this "the connections game." See if you can identify mutual acquaintances. Playing the connections game can be an important contribution to the interview. Not only will this allow you to get to know the candidate better, but it also may provide leads for follow-up conversations with others who know the candidate.

2. *What do you like to do for fun? Are you a sports fan? Do you like music? What kind of music do you enjoy? What are your favorite movies or books? What do you and your family do for fun?* All these questions are valid. Of course, there are obviously not any right or wrong answers to these questions—provided he is not a Yankees fan! The point of these kinds of questions is to get to know a candidate's personality and consider whether or not he might have some "chemistry" with your particular church. Don't hesitate to spend time on questions like these.

3. *Tell us about your decision to enter vocational Christian ministry.* When you ask a candidate to tell the story of his "calling," be looking for answers that communicate that it was indeed God who called him into ministry. This call

should be evident not only in an inward confidence on the part of the candidate that God has called him, but also in the affirmation of local churches that have affirmed this man's gifts and qualification for ministry.

4. *Tell us about the community and church where you currently serve. What have you learned about your current context that helps you shepherd your particular flock?* The candidate's answers to this should demonstrate that he is a student of the people and of the place where he serves. Even if he isn't currently serving as a pastor, he should still be able to cite some evidence that demonstrates he has been sensitive to the setting in which he currently finds himself.

5. *Briefly, summarize for us the gospel and why it is the greatest news ever heard.* This may seem basic. And it is. For any pastor called to pastoral ministry, this should be a belt-high fastball that he hits into the upper deck. A candidate should be able to express concisely what *gospel* means—"good news"—and that it is centered on the Lord Jesus Christ. Watch to see whether the candidate references such clear passages as 1 Corinthians 15:1–3 or the gospel of John. Ideally, candidates should be able to outline why the gospel has implications not only for a believer's relationship with God, but also for all of life.

6. *How has your education prepared you to preach on a weekly basis?* The skills to prepare a sermon are not developed in hours. They must be learned and honed

across the years. The search committee must evaluate whether a candidate has been continually cultivating the necessary tools and experience to prepare a Word-centered sermon, week in and week out.

The candidate's educational background will have been a vital part of his formation. The ideal seminary degrees are a master of divinity (MDiv) degree or, a step further, a master of theology (ThM) degree. In many seminaries, these require that the student will have studied the original biblical languages in addition to biblical and systematic theology. These MDiv and ThM degrees are designed for the express purpose of preparing the individual for the pastorate. The standard accreditation association for seminaries is the Association of Theological Schools (ATS; see www.ats.edu). You can check the ATS website to see whether a particular seminary is accredited. There *are* solid seminaries that are *not* ATS-accredited. But you may want to investigate further if the seminary does not have this accreditation.

Don't automatically rule someone out who *does not* have a seminary degree. I know more than one effective pastor who does not have a seminary degree. Even C. H. Spurgeon—"the Prince of Preachers"—had no seminary degree! If a candidate does not have a seminary degree, you will need to evaluate the level of motivation he has shown in studying on his own. Look at what he has done so far. Is there concrete evidence that this is one of those rare men who are committed, self-disciplined, and self-motivated enough to prepare themselves for ministry without formal theological education?

7. *Are you ordained?* If the answer is yes, then ask the interviewee to describe the process he went through in order to be ordained. Not all ordinations are equal. Nowadays, it is possible to get ordained over the Internet! So be sure to ask questions. If the candidate wrote a doctrinal statement for ordination, then ask if he is willing to share a copy of it (and any other written materials that were given to the ordaining body) that would be appropriate for you to see.

8. *Tell us about a difficult time in your life and how God used that time to better equip you for pastoral ministry.* One of the foundational ways that God prepares leaders is through trials. As J. Oswald Sanders has written, "When a man is really marked out by God for leadership, He will see to it that he receives the necessary disciplines to make him effective."[1] You will learn a great deal about a candidate's preparation for pastoral ministry if you listen to him describe how he has been broken and matured through trials.

9. *When your work wears you down, in what ways do you seek renewal for ministry?* Ministry is exhausting. A pastor who does not know how to recharge his batteries may burn out. Don't be impressed by a pastor who says that he never takes time off. This is not a good thing.

10. *Have you read our church's doctrinal statement? Would you say it aligns with your own doctrine? If you were to*

change anything about our church's statement of faith, what would it be? Church doctrinal statements are not part of the inspired Word of God. So if a candidate responds with something like, "I might make the paragraph on end times a little less restrictive," this does not mean that you should immediately rule him out. But the candidate must wholeheartedly support the core doctrines of Scripture and be committed to your church's ongoing faithful adherence to those core doctrines.

11. *How have you shown to the people you lead that you love and care for them? Would you say that communicating your love is a strong point for you?* The Good Shepherd laid down His life for the sheep. Pastors must communicate to their people that they love them and care about them. Of course, different personalities do this in different ways. But the flock must have some confidence that their shepherd loves them, that he is striving to model Christ's unconditional, self-sacrificial love.

12. *What do you see about our church and community that would indicate to you that God might indeed be calling you as the best fit to be our pastor?* Listen for evidence that the pastor understands he cannot simply come to your church and repeat whatever he has done elsewhere. He will need to listen carefully, study, and understand your church, its history, and the community where it is found, and so forth.

13. *When was the last time someone confronted you about an area where you need to grow or where you offended them? How did you respond?* Be prepared to follow up with more questions.

14. *Do you tend to avoid conflict; or, on the other hand, do you tend to be too confrontational? Would you share with us an example of a time when you exhorted someone in the right way?*

15. *Can you tell us about a time that you counseled someone struggling with a particular sin problem, such as a man in your church who indicated that he is struggling with Internet pornography? Tell us about how you worked through this.* Pastors should demonstrate an ability to bring the Word to bear in counseling situations. Ideally, candidates would answer this question by talking about some basic counseling principles. This would include trying to understand if the counselee truly shows evidence of being a Christian, the circumstances in which the problem has developed, what Scriptures would be relevant to the particular situation, why it is urgent that the problem be addressed, what strategy should be implemented for working through the problem, why there is hope through the gospel of the Lord Jesus Christ, and the sort of homework that pastors should give to someone struggling.

16. *Have you officiated at wedding ceremonies? How do you make decisions about whether or not to do a wedding?*

What do you require of couples that you marry? Pastors should talk about how they make decisions about weddings and also their approach to premarital counseling.

17. *Have you led funeral services? Talk to us about how you have served a family during a funeral. How do you go about it?* If the candidate has not yet done funerals, ask if he has a plan for how to approach them. His answer should include principles for how a pastor should deal with those who are grieving, but also what a pastor should keep in mind when doing a funeral service. This subject can easily be followed up with a question about how a funeral should be approached for an unbeliever. You might also ask how the pastor approaches doing funerals for people whom he does not know.

18. *How do you keep organized for ministry? Talk to us about how you maintain your calendar, your approach to filing material for sermons, and your systems for filing in general.* Your next pastor doesn't have to be strongly administrative. But he ought to value administration and organization. If interviewees say they are neither administrative nor organized, that is okay. But you should see solid evidence that they recognize the need for organization, that they strive to compensate for their weaknesses, and that they seek to involve people who are gifted in these areas to assist them. The demands of pastoral ministry require organization. Pastors cannot effectively shepherd if they do not have a

system for keeping track of the flock (Proverbs 27:23–24). As J. Oswald Sanders stated succinctly, "The lazy and disorganized never rise to true leadership."[2]

Questions to Evaluate Whether the Candidate Is Committed to Biblical Preaching

1. *What is your philosophy or theology of preaching?* Look for a candidate to derive from the Word of God his conclusions about preaching the Word of God. It should be clear that he believes the Bible is God's Word, that it is useful for teaching, rebuking, correcting, and training in righteousness. He should also assert that preaching is God's appointed means for feeding His people. You would also be listening for something about how God gave His Word to reveal Himself, how it is a written reflection of Jesus Christ the Living Word, and how the Holy Spirit works in and through the preaching of the Word.

2. *What biblical passages on preaching have influenced your approach to preaching?* Ideally, the candidate will make this question obsolete by covering it in his answer to the previous question. Any theology of preaching should be built upon the Word. However, if he fails to point you to an explicit passage, give him a chance. Rephrase it to try to draw out whatever biblical basis he may have, such as, "What passages that talk about God's Word and preaching have become especially meaningful to you?"

   If I were in a candidate's shoes again, I would answer

this question by first establishing our fundamental need to *hear from God*. Passages like Deuteronomy 8:1–12, Psalm 19, Proverbs 29:18 and Matthew 4:4 make this point that we must have revelation about God's character and work from God Himself. From there, I would stress that today God speaks to His people through His inspired Word (2 Timothy 3:16–17). And I would point out that the first thing that Paul says to Timothy after he emphasizes the inspiration of Scripture is that those called to the pulpit must *preach the Word* (2 Timothy 4:1–4).

There are many passages to which a candidate might turn. Most of all, you want to make sure that his view of preaching is indeed based on the Bible and that he can show you from Scripture why he believes what he does about preaching.

3. *What well-known preachers do you hold in high regard?* There are many solid preachers. Maybe the men whose preaching has most profoundly influenced the candidate are not well-known. Be open to that possibility. But any potential pastor for your church ought to be a student both of preaching and of other preachers. If you are unfamiliar with the preachers your candidate mentions, you may want to obtain one or two of those preachers' recordings.

4. *What constitutes a good sermon?* The long answer to this question appears in chapters 6 to 9. The person you are interviewing may not word it the same way, but

look for some like-mindedness. At the very least, he should say something about God's Word coming to bear on lives through the power of the Holy Spirit. It may help you when you consider an answer to this question to have the sermon evaluation form on hand for quick reference.

Can the Candidate Deliver a Word-Honoring Sermon?

Does the candidate understand the process that preparing a message requires and live it out in sermon preparation? Your goal will be to ask questions organized around each of the five steps of preparing an expository sermon, described in chapter 6.

1. *If you preach topically, how do you select passages to support your points?* A *topical* sermon (i.e., a sermon deliberately prepared about a certain subject or to address a selected issue) can be preached expositionally. Some people believe that the categories of "topical" and "expository" preaching are mutually exclusive. But either one of those kinds of sermons can be characterized by faithful exegesis, righteous handling of the selected biblical texts.

   In previous chapters, I've explained how Word-centered preaching is preaching that exalts what God has revealed rather than man's opinions and private interpretations. In other words, pastors and students of the Scriptures have a responsibility to derive meaning and conclusions from God's Word rather than imposing their own meaning and conclusions upon it. Pastors should exposit God's Word—and that doesn't mean just going through a passage word by word and line by line with detailed overanalysis. We should not read into the text what we would like for it to say (called *eisegesis*), but we should commit ourselves to faithful study and relaying of what God actually says in His Word (called *exegesis*).

I occasionally preach a series of sermons on a particular topic because as a pastor I believe that my flock needs to have a better grasp of it. But my topical sermons are still prepared and delivered expositionally. For example, I have preached a series on the topic of "forgiveness." I laid out my game plan ahead of time, I chose a different passage that dealt with forgiveness and preached through a different passage each week for a month. My messages were derived from the following passages:

Summary of a Topical Sermon Series
That Was Presented Expositionally

Week #	Passage
1	Ephesians 4:32—*"Be kind and compassionate to one another, forgiving each other, just as in Christ God forgave you."* (NIV)
2	Matthew 18:21–35—*The parable of the unmerciful servant*
3	Proverbs 19:11— *"A man's wisdom gives him patience, it is to his glory to overlook an offense."* (NIV)

4 Romans 12:17–21— *"Repay no one evil for evil. . . . If possible, so far as it depends on you, live peaceably with all. . . . Do not be overcome by evil, but overcome evil with good."*

So do not allow yourselves to be alarmed if the candidate "admits to" preaching topical sermons on occasion. His doing so demonstrates that he strives as a shepherd to stay attuned to the particular needs of his particular flock. And his preaching topically does not mean necessarily that he drops the ball when it comes to Word-honoring exegesis. That's why it is important to quiz him on how he goes about preparing and delivering a topical sermon. Ask him questions along these lines: "Do you usually begin your preparation with a passage you would like to preach? Or do you tend more often to select a particular issue or theme, and then find passages that address that issue or theme?"

2. *How far in advance do you prefer to plan your sermons?* Ideally, a preacher should know generally where he is going with his preaching for at least the next year. Without a general "lesson plan" in place for the year, it is very difficult to collect material and properly study amid all the other demands of pastoral ministry. Further, there is great benefit in knowing your goals and direction for the pulpit ministry, so that other Bible studies and Christian education programs within a local church can be coordinated to coincide with the sermons.

3. *Could you give an overview of one or more sermon series that you have preached?* Some pastors may never preach sermon series. Personally, I think it is important. Either way, you should be aware of the candidate's preferences and views on preaching through series. If the candidate does preach through series, follow this question up by asking how he decided upon and developed the series, planned it, did any relevant artwork, etc.

4. *Do you develop your own messages, or do you re-preach others' sermons, or borrow from material that someone else has prepared?* There is a wide range of opinions about what should be considered an acceptable answer to this question on a few levels—including legality, ethics, and responsibility (i.e., the extent to which you are comfortable with a pastor on your payroll pulling from other resources rather than relying upon his own study). The matter of sharing sermon content is one of degrees and is complicated, because some well-known pastors permit and encourage others to use their materials without giving credit. One pastor recently lost his job because he was using someone else's materials and disagreed with other church leaders about what constitutes plagiarism.

5. *How important do you believe it is in preaching to focus a sermon on one central thought or "big idea"?* If the candidate you are interviewing has studied homiletics, then he will usually own the importance of having a clearly stated central proposition. In the event that he

does not see this as significant and best, you would be well advised to evaluate his sermons and see whether they are organized and focused. You may find that his sermons ramble from one thought to another. Even if this sounds okay at first, over time he will probably tend to go back to the same soapbox rather than allowing the truth of God's Word to speak in a fresh way today.

6. *How do you make sure that your sermon speaks to a wide range of people?* There could be many different approaches to ensuring this. Many preachers try to picture a diversity of different people during sermon preparation. This is something I often do. The bottom line is that in order to preach "a biblical bullet into the life of a believer," the pastor will need to be involved in some way in people's lives.

7. *In what area(s) would you say that your preaching needs to grow?* Remember, other than our Lord, there has never been a perfect preacher. All of us should be able to point to areas where we need to grow. If the candidate points to some technical aspect of preaching like, "I need to work on my conclusions," this would provide insight that not only does he understand preaching, but also that he is thinking about how to improve and grow. Over the last several years of evaluating my own preaching, I have become convinced that my conclusions need work. I have thought carefully about how to improve them.

8. *What do you consider to be your greatest strength as a preacher?* Every candidate will answer this one differently. The answer may provide insight into the candidate's personality and personal character (his shyness, his prejudices, "people skills," his humility, honesty, understanding of self), as well as insight into his priorities (his passions, his ideas of shepherding responsibilities, etc.).

A Key Component of the Interview

I don't want to seem too cynical, but allow me to conclude this section with a couple of paragraphs from John Grisham's novel *The Firm*. This exchange is part of an interview in the first section:

> "You've done quite well here, Mitch," Mr. Lambert said, admiring the résumé. The dossier was in the briefcase, under the table.
>
> "Thank you. I've worked hard."
>
> "You made extremely high grades in your tax and securities courses."
>
> "That's where my interest lies."
>
> "We've reviewed your writing sample, and it's quite impressive."
>
> "Thank you. I enjoy research."
>
> They nodded and acknowledged this obvious lie. It was part of the ritual. No law student or lawyer in his right mind enjoyed research, yet, without fail,

every prospective associate professed a deep love for the library.[3]

I would not want to imply in any way that we should assume the worst about a candidate, that he would lie about his preaching. However, part of the "ritual" in this business of seeking a pastorate has become that most pastors will emphasize a love for study and sermon preparation. They may even mean this sincerely. However, your job as a search committee is to evaluate as objectively as possible how well the reality of the candidate's ministry matches up with his claims. If he asserts that he enjoys sermon preparation and that he is committed to conscientious preparation, your committee must evaluate whether his assertions truly are consistent with his past track record, present habits, and future intentions. A careful interview is key in ascertaining the reality accurately.

NOTES

1. J Oswald Sanders, *Spiritual Leadership* (Chicago: Moody, 1994) 184.
2. Ibid., 67.
3. John Grisham, *The Firm* (New York: Doubleday, 1991), 5.

BUT AFTER ALL, the grand secret is habitually to have our eye upon Christ. Peter—looking at the waves instead of the Saviour—"began to sink." We too—if we look at the difficulties of our work, and forgetting the upholding arm of our ever present Head—shall sink in despondency.

Charles Bridges
The Christian Ministry

THE LORD IS WITH YOU while you are with him. If you seek him, he will be found by you, but if you forsake him, he will forsake you.

2 Chronicles 15:1–2

Conclusion: Not in Our Strength

As a future pastor in seminary, I began wondering how I would shepherd people through deep valleys that come with the changing seasons of life. One of my seminary professors once told a story about a family that faced a terrible tragedy. I asked him, "How do you minister to someone in that situation?" I'll never forget his answer. He looked me square in the eye and said, "If you never did anything in advance to prepare them, there is relatively little you can do at the time."

His reply has echoed in my thoughts for years. Each Sunday when a pastor preaches, he is called to prepare his people for times of weeping and laughing, mourning and dancing. If the Word is not preached, if the flock is not shepherded, then they will not be prepared. It is a job of supreme significance.

And so, in calling a pastor, your church has a great opportunity to make a difference. Your charge means more than any corporate search for a new CEO. Your search committee meetings in living rooms and church basements weigh heavier on the scales of eternity than those held on the ninetieth floor of high rises to discuss global mergers.

Ask yourselves, "How many lives will be impacted and for how long?" Week in, week out, your new pastor will proclaim the truth. He will preach funerals for the unchurched and offer the good news to those who have not heard it. He will encourage widows who miss their husbands. He will serve communion. He will preach to teenagers and their parents, new wives and their husbands, singles and empty nesters. Most weeks, you will listen to him preach at least once.

You may respond, "Thanks a lot for ending your book by turning up the pressure for those of us who are leading the search." My response to that would be, "It's good to understand the weight of the responsibility, but you don't need to do it in your strength." Rather, look to Christ and His Word. Let Him lead your search. We don't have to rely on ourselves.

At the beginning of this book I confessed I was never any good at dating. And, seriously, I wasn't. But I looked for a wife in a Word-centered way. I got involved in a local church where the Word of God was consistently proclaimed. I was part of an adult Bible fellowship and I studied the Word of God. I prayed fervently. And God blessed. I met my wife, Jamie, at church and she is a greater blessing than I ever could have imagined. Some of you no doubt have the same testimonies about your marriages.

The same can be true in your search for a pastor. If you pursue a pastor in a Word-centered way, then you can prayerfully look forward to God's blessing, not because of who you are, but because of who God is. "For the eyes of the Lord run to and fro throughout the whole earth, to give strong support to those whose heart is blameless toward him" (2 Chronicles 16:9).

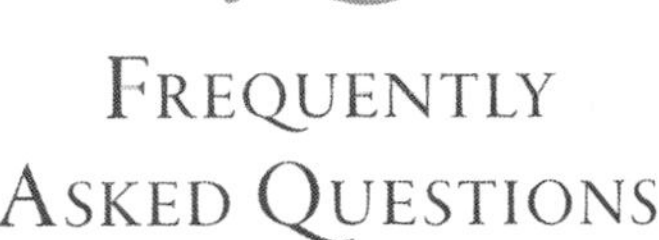

Frequently Asked Questions

If you buy books like I buy them, then this may be one of the first sections you scan when deciding whether to purchase the book. I can't be too critical of this approach given the beam in my own eye. Still, I would caution you that parts 1 and 2 really survey the key Bible themes that churches looking for a pastor should consider. This is just the preview. Indeed, you will see that in several of the answers that follow, I point you back to earlier chapters.

Some of the answers may help you think procedurally about calling a pastor. As I stated in the introduction, this is not a procedural guide; other resources provide that. But this will help you anticipate some of the common questions your leadership will face as you search for your next pastor.

A good first question is, "What are the mistakes we should avoid when looking for a pastor?" Knowing the mistakes churches make can help your church to avoid them. Turn the page to find the ten common mistakes churches make while searching for a pastor; keep turning to find the answers to nine other frequently asked questions.

- **What are common mistakes that churches make looking for a pastor?**

1. *Not choosing the right people for the pastoral search committee.* See Part 1, all four chapters. For the optimal size for a pastoral search committee, see FAQ 2.
2. *Prayerlessness.* No Bible believing church would admit that they don't think prayer is important. But the reality of what many do makes that statement. See chapter 1.
3. *Being people-centered rather than Word-centered.* See chapter 2.
4. *Lack of follow-through and due-diligence by the pastoral search committee.* See chapter 4.
5. *Impatience that leads to the wrong decision.* See next page.
6. *Failure to properly administrate the pastoral search.* See next page.
7. *Inadequate communication.* See page 174.
8. *Failure to adequately budget for the pastoral search.* See page 175.
9. *Allowing the experience with the previous pastor to direct the calling of the next pastor.* See page 176.
10. *Spending too much time trying to call pastors who are not "reasonably gettable."* Tim Keller would probably do a good job as your next pastor. But unless you are in Redeemer Presbyterian Church

in New York, the odds are that he isn't going to accept a call. Look for someone who is a good fit in your church and community.

Avoiding Mistake #5—*Impatience that leads to the wrong decision*. It is not uncommon for pastoral searches to last two years or more. Therefore, it is important from the beginning that leaders encourage the church that they will need to be patient.

The patience of a church can be stretched very thin if a promising candidate asks for his name to be removed or the pastoral search committee decides to not go forward with that candidate for one reason or another. This is not uncommon. More often than not, churches looking for a pastor go through at least one major disappointment when they believe they have found the right pastor but for one reason or another it does not work out. If this happens to your church, don't make a mistake in the wake of that disappointment and rush a decision.

If you do find that your congregation is struggling with impatience, encourage them to elevate their thoughts of God and wait on Him. Meditate on Isaiah 40:28–31, resting in the truth that "the everlasting God . . . does not faint or grow weary; his understanding is unsearchable." Be confident that God will work at His appointed season (Titus 1:3). Rest in the confidence that if you wait for the Lord, He will renew your strength.

Avoiding Mistake #6—*Failure to properly administrate the pastoral search*. Appoint or, preferably, hire someone to be in charge of administration for the search. Tommy Thomas explains:

> Every search needs someone with strong administrative skills who has time to devote to the administrative and follow-up activities of a search. This must be someone who has the confidence of the members of the search committee because ultimately this person will be handling a lot of highly confidential matters.[1]

Consider how much information you will handle. You will need to keep track of résumés, correspondence, sermons, and background checks. Further, your pastoral search committee will need to hold one another accountable for completing assignments such as listening to sermons, contacting candidates, or contacting references.

Avoiding Mistake #7—*Inadequate communication.* Leaders must communicate often with the congregation during a pastoral search. Given that one of the challenges of the pastoral search is remaining patient, if you give written updates to your church on at least a monthly basis, then this will encourage your flock that the process is moving forward.

Your church will be well served if you appoint someone with excellent skills in written communication to be in charge of drafting written communication to both the congregation and to candidates.

Your elders and pastoral search committee should not

feel obligated to share specific information about candidates with the congregation. It will be important for the pastoral search committee to keep information confidential. Indeed, one of the first things your pastoral search committee should do is to review the importance of confidentiality.

Avoiding Mistake #8—*Failure to adequately budget for the pastoral search*. Recognize going in that there are significant costs for looking for a new pastor. But it is worth spending the money. Spending 20 to 40 percent of the pastor's annual compensation and benefits package, or even more, is a wise investment if it helps you make a quality decision. The cost of a poor decision cannot be quantified. But when you consider needing to do another pastoral search, a poor decision could easily cost two to three times the pastor's annual compensation and benefits.

Some of the costs you may encounter would include: travel expenses for your pastoral search committee, travel expenses for pastoral candidates, honorariums for pastoral candidates, honorariums for association or denomination leaders who assist your church, advertising of the position, development of printed and video materials that describe your church, and search firms or consultants. You also need to anticipate relocation costs.

Remember, calling a pastor is a two-way street. It is not simply his responsibility to persuade your church that he should be your pastor. You want to persuade a quality candidate that your church would be a wise investment of his life. Putting your best foot forward in every way will require an adequate budget.

Avoiding Mistake #9—*Allowing the experience with the previous pastor to direct the calling of the next pastor.* Many if not most churches tend to hire out of a reaction to the previous pastor. They look for a pastor who will be strong in areas where the previous pastor was weak, or perceived as weak. At the same time, they assume that the next pastor will have the strengths of the previous pastor. Of course, you cannot help but be affected in some ways by your previous experience with a pastor. But make it your goal to be Word-centered in hiring your next pastor rather than centered in your experience.

There also are times when the previous pastor was highly respected, and the church is looking for someone who is like him. If this means looking for a pastor who preaches the Word and is a biblical shepherd, then it is a good thing. However, be careful not to confuse style with biblical qualifications. Don't make it your goal to look for a pastor who is stylistically like the previous pastor. Whether it was a negative or positive, your experience with the previous pastor should not become the defining force for calling your next pastor.

• How large should the pastoral search committee be?

There are different opinions about the ideal size for the group leading the pastoral search; somewhere in the range of six to ten people is probably best. There is too much work for a smaller group. And it is hard to get quality interaction from everyone in larger groups.

If the elders of your church do not serve as the pastoral

search committee, then be sure the pastoral search committee has received a clear charge in writing so that they know what is expected and how they should relate to the board.

- **Should the church pay the candidate's expenses when we do an interview?**

Yes. Ask the candidate to keep receipts and reimburse him accordingly, including mileage preferably at the allowable rate set by the Internal Revenue Service. Of course, you should give an honorarium whenever you have someone fill the pulpit who is not your pastor.

- **We have a number of experienced people in our church; can we do the search without any outside help?**

Probably not. Don't forget the Bereans, who were humble and teachable (see pages 59–61). It is almost always a good idea to take advantage of the wisdom of people outside your local church. For one thing, they will be able to look at your situation more objectively and advise you accordingly. Further, you will be able to take advantage of people who spend far more time thinking biblically about pastoral placement.

If you are in a denomination or association of churches that value biblical preaching, then I encourage you to seek help from one of your association leaders. Helping churches through transitions is usually a major part of their job description. Even if you do not agree with these larger groups in every aspect, surely you can glean some valuable insight and maybe even some potential candidates' contact information thanks to larger groups' experience, affiliations, and connections.

You might also ask a pastor or a seminary professor to help you interview candidates about doctrinal questions. It is interesting to note that most churches would not dream of conducting a doctrinal examination for an ordination on their own without outside pastors' participation. Yet, ironically, churches do assume they are up for examining pastoral candidates on their own. Why not ask for outside help to examine candidates theologically?

If the option of denomination or association help is not available to your church, or if you prefer to work outside your own network, you might retain a consultant or search firm. At first it may seem like a lot of money, but remember what is at stake. The decision is so important, the cost so small relative to what we as a church invest in pastors, that it would be well worth the cost to obtain some clear analysis of the sermons submitted by potential candidates.

The calling of a preaching pastor is the most strategic decision that a local church makes. A search firm offers the opportunity to temporarily expand the size of your staff. They will bring particular expertise in the area of pastoral searches so that you do not lean too much on your experience with secular searches. Search firms are also valuable because candidates and those giving referrals trust them to maintain confidentiality.[2]

- **Where will we find names or contacts?**

One approach I would recommend is to contact several pastors who know your church and who are committed to being biblical pastors. Ask them to help you network and find a pastor who is available.[3]

It may also be that your association or denomination has a system whereby you can find the names of candidates who may be a fit for your local church.

You might also advertise your need on a website such as www.churchstaffing.com. If you choose this approach, be prepared to be inundated with a large number of résumés.

- **Should pastoral search committees move forward only if they are unanimous?**

Be careful of establishing a ground rule that your pastoral search committee must be completely unanimous. Of course, there needs to be a strong consensus from the pastoral search committee. But a requirement of unanimity might create a scenario where one difficult pastoral search committee member can prevent the church from moving forward with a qualified candidate.

- **Biblically, what should we keep in mind when putting together a compensation package?**

One of the ways the Bible motivates you as a believer to support your pastor is by teaching that it is in your own best interest to do so. Look out for your pastor and you are looking out for yourself.

Think of it this way. When I got my first car, my dad immediately began teaching me that clean oil prolongs the life of an engine. I've never met a mechanic who disagreed. My dad didn't tell me to change the oil because he worshiped the vehicle that I drove. Even if I had driven a Maserati that did 185 mph, which I didn't, concern for the car wasn't his basic concern. My dad was looking out for his son. He told me to service my car because it was a machine that served me.

The Bible uses similar reasoning to motivate people to take care of their pastors. Paul compared caring for the pastor to taking care of oxen—the ancient Near East equivalent of engines. Paul told Timothy, "The elders who direct the affairs of the church well are worthy of double honor, especially those whose work is preaching and teaching. For the Scripture says, 'Do not muzzle the ox while it is treading out the grain'" (1 Timothy 5:17–18 NIV).

In other words, think of your pastor as an engine that serves you. Supporting your pastor is really about taking care of yourself. Take care of your pastor. It is in your interest to do so. He is the engine that drives the spiritual lives in your church and community.

- **What areas should be included in the compensation package?**

I strongly recommend that two or three leaders familiarize themselves with basic principles of clergy compensation. Keep in mind that the tax laws are quite different for clergy.

When it is time to extend a call to a candidate, write a detailed letter that spells out the compensation package that you are offering. This should include your church's approach to: base salary, housing allowance, retirement, book allowance, budget for ongoing education or conference expenses, if babysitting for church events will be reimbursed for pastors with young children, mileage at the Internal Revenue Service allowable rate, expenses for meals related to pastoral duty, phone expenses, computer, health insurance, disability, and life insurance.

You should also specify the number of vacation weeks allowed and how many Sundays this includes, ministry time, or how often he will be permitted to be away to speak or minister elsewhere, and how many Sundays he is expected to preach each year.

Specify how you will help with relocation expenses.

- **How much vacation time should a compensation package include?**

Be sure to be generous with vacation and study time. You may be tempted to say something like, "When I started at my job, I didn't get more than one or two weeks of vacation for some number of years." When I worked in the corporate world, I received two weeks of vacation. However, bear in mind that in pastoral ministry, the pastor's vocational life, social network, and spiritual life are all centered in the church. This, along with the spiritual battle of the Christian life, makes it wise to give pastors more vacation than they might receive in a secular position. In addition, it is healthy for the congregation to hear others proclaim the Word.

• Is preaching really that important?

In contrast to other resources written for pastoral search committees, I have placed a great emphasis on preaching. Looking at that emphasis, some may say, "Do you think you have overemphasized the preaching of the Word?" In responding to this question, let me make two final points.

First, if your pastor is godly, you can shore up his weaknesses in every area but preaching. If a pastor lacks administrative gifts and skills, you can put people around him who help in that area. Or, if like me, he is not musical, you can make sure he has plenty of assistance there. But if he preaches and is not gifted to preach, then it is going to be a tough go.

Of course, this doesn't mean that you should expect your pastor to preach like Spurgeon. Thankfully, my church doesn't require that. It does mean that you should look for a pastor who will, "Clearly fire a biblical bullet at the life of the listener."

Second, the Bible prescribes that the preaching of the Word be central in the life of the church. When I first started at the church where I now serve, one of our people commented that preaching need not be a central activity at church each week. She was very affirming about my preaching, and the e-mail was sweet in tone, but her thought was that we could use our Sunday morning worship service for other activities on certain weeks. She was thinking specifically of prayer and the children singing.

Rather than feeling defensive about her suggestion, I began asking our people why we preach the Word on Sunday morning. I asked this in a couple of different settings. The answers were all very similar. They responded that we need preaching in order to grow, to be taught, to learn God's Word. Some stressed evangelism. Others brought up the ongoing growth of believers.

The answers they gave were not bad answers. God does use preaching to accomplish these things. But there was a glaring absence in the responses. None of these people really got to the heart of the matter: Preaching is God's specifically appointed means for the proclamation of His Word. God does not tell Timothy or Titus, "Preach the Word, have plenty of music, and by all means get the children involved." He does not say that drama should be rotated in with preaching. I am not categorically opposed to drama. But Paul, writing under the inspiration of the Holy Spirit, stresses that the center of what pastors are called to do is preach the Word, in season and out of season, week in, and week out.

If Sunday is only about imparting content, then this could be accomplished through preaching and also through other means. If the reason that we have preaching on Sunday mornings is simply so that God's people can grow, then we might set up interactive computer programs and have people work through guided learning. We might provide reading assignments or do drama exclusively. The fact is that God specifically tells pastors to preach the Word. While we may choose at times to do other activities, they cannot replace preaching. Nothing can.

Different church strategies and fads will come and go. Adult Bible Fellowships may work well during one generation. The next may focus on small groups. A church may choose to do a bus ministry or start a Christian school. Such programs are fine and even necessary. But until Christ comes back, local churches are called to feature a clear and powerful proclamation of the Word of God.

Just remember: *Biblical preaching is central and vital to the life of a local church*. Both the content and the means are important. God's chosen means for feeding His people is through the preaching of the Word. If you believe that, you must do everything you can as search committees to equip yourselves to evaluate preaching and call the right preaching pastor. Indeed, serving on a pastoral search committee is a most strategic call.

Notes

1. Tommy W. Thomas, *The Perfect Search* (Grand Rapids: Credo House, 2009), 16–17.
2. My thanks to Tom Boyce for his thoughts on the value of search firms.
3. My thanks to Dr. Albert Mohler for his input on this question.

Recommended Reading

By listing a source in this section, I do not mean to imply that I am in complete agreement with everything in that source. It is necessary to maintain a Berean attitude and apply it especially to the writings of human beings. "But test everything; hold fast what is good" (1 Thessalonians 5:21; cf. Acts 17:11).

FORMING THE PASTORAL SEARCH COMMITTEE

The following books focus on procedure or the actual steps taken to call a pastor and are helpful in that regard. They spend very little time considering biblical teaching about the pastoral office or how to evaluate preaching.

An asterisk (*) designates one of the three books I would recommend reading *first* among the recommended books for forming pastoral search committees.

Dingman, Robert W. *In Search of a Leader: The Complete Search Committee Guidebook*. Ventura, Calif.: Regal, 1989.

Dingman heads his own executive search firm. This book is helpful with the process and procedures of calling a leader, although not with surveying what the Bible teaches about shepherding and preaching.

Foose, Dean E. *Searching for a Pastor the Presbyterian Way: A Roadmap for Pastor Nominating Committees.* Louisville: Geneva, 2001.
The book identifies Foose as a Presbyterian minister who served as the director of alumni relations and placement at Princeton Theological Seminary. This book may be helpful from a process or procedures standpoint, especially for Presbyterians.

*Moberg, Ken. *Ask . . . Seek . . . Knock: A Step-by-Step Guide for Pastoral Transitions.* Minneapolis: EFCA Publications, 2009.
Moberg is a district leader for the Evangelical Free Church of America. His objective is to write a step-by-step guide for the process of calling a pastor. A CD is available that supplements this book. It provides sample letters and other documents that pastoral search committees can adapt for their own purposes. Overall, this book is a very helpful resource.

*Thomas, Tommy W. *The Perfect Search.* Grand Rapids: Credo House, 2009.
The author has decades of experience with an executive search firm. Thomas takes his wisdom in the field of human resources and brings it to bear on a search for just the right leader. Many of the principles in areas such as "behavioral interviewing" will be helpful to pastoral search committees. This book does not specifically target pastoral searches and so makes no attempt to interact with biblical teaching.

Umidi, Joseph L. *Confirming the Pastoral Call: A Guide to Matching Candidates and Congregations.* Grand Rapids: Kregel, 2000.

Umidi argues that churches will call the right pastor by making *the right match*. In order to call the right pastor, local churches need to discover who they are as a church, and understand a potential pastor, so that they can pair the right church with the right pastor. This is accomplished through "values discovery." This book is helpful, though one wishes there was an emphasis on *teaching the congregation biblical truth* rather than simply discovering the values already present.

*Virkler, Henry A. *Choosing a New Pastor: The Complete Handbook*. Nashville: Nelson, 1992.

This is a general resource for pastoral search committees that will help committee members with the process and procedures of calling a pastor, though not with biblical teaching. Virkler provides a helpful summary of mistakes that pastoral search committees often make.

Weese, Carolyn, and J. Russell Crabtree. *The Elephant in the Boardroom*. San Francisco: Jossey-Bass, 2004.

Weese and Crabtree's goal is to encourage churches to plan for a transition from their current pastor. It is written from a business management point of view. This book may be better suited for large churches. It encourages churches to have a transition plan before it is needed.

DETERMINING COMPENSATION AND BENEFITS

Every church needs to understand the proper way to put together a compensation package for the pastor. The resources from *Church Law Today* are thorough and very helpful.

Hammar, Richard. *2010 Church and Clergy Tax Guide, 2010.*

This book is a tremendous resource for understanding how to put together a new pastor's compensation package, and for how different tax laws apply to your church. It is published by *Church Law Today* and is available from http://store.churchlawtodaystore.com/.

The 2010-2011 Compensation Handbook for Church Staff.

This handbook shares a salary survey broken down by a number of different factors, including church size, income, budget, and geographical setting. It is published by *Church Law Today* and is available from http://store.churchlawtodaystore.com.

Rickard, James. *The Pastor and His Salary Package.* Schaumburg, Ill.: Regular Baptist Press, 2009.

Rickard has decades of experience with determining pastoral compensation; and this is a concise and helpful article on the topic. Available from http://www.baptistbulletin.org/?p=2223.

BEING UNIFIED AND RESOLVING CONFLICT

Unfortunately, it is often true that churches are looking for a pastor because the previous pastor left amid conflict. If true healing is to take place, then biblical principles of forgiveness and peacemaking must be implemented before the pastoral search can advance in a Word-centered way.

Braun, Chris. *Unpacking Forgiveness: Biblical Answers for Complex Questions and Deep Wounds.* Wheaton, Ill.: Crossway, 2008.

Unpacking Forgiveness is intended to be a resource for local churches working through conflict. I pray that the chapter, "What If Christians Cannot Agree?" will be helpful to many churches who have been forced to say good-bye to a pastor in the midst of conflict.

Dever, Mark. *What Is a Healthy Church?* Wheaton, Ill.: Crossway, 2007.

This is an affordable, brief, and readable introduction to biblical teaching about the local church. It makes an ideal study for churches in transition who wish to reestablish a New Testament vision for a healthy local church.

________. *Twelve Challenges Churches Face.* Wheaton, Ill.: Crossway, 2008.

First Corinthians was written to a very conflicted church. Dever's expositional thoughts show how being

Christ- and Cross-centered can help a church move forward together in a unified way.

Sande, Ken. *The Peace Maker.* Grand Rapids: Baker, 2004. Reprint, 3rd.
If I could recommend only one resource on working through conflicts, it would be Ken Sande's *The Peace Maker.* It contains a wealth of practical information on how to work through conflict resolution. Sande and the organization he founded, Peacemaker Ministries, have decades of experience in working through conflict resolution, and this book is a gold mine of practical advice. See also www.hispeace.org.

EVALUATING PREACHING

This book has argued for the foundational importance of preaching. If you wish to learn more about biblical preaching, the below books offer a good beginning point.

If you are *not* looking for a textbook on preaching, but *do* want to grow in understanding why preaching is so central in the life of the church, then begin with Mohler's book. T. David Gordon's book is concise and will also be a direct help to pastoral search committees. An asterisk (*) designates the three books I would recommend reading *first* among the recommended books for evaluating preaching.

Azurdia, Arturo G. *Spirit Empowered Preaching: Involving the Holy Spirit in Your Ministry.* Geanies House, Scotland: Mentor, Christian Focus Publications, 1998.

If you wish to learn more about how a sermon should be "fired," i.e., a sermon that is preached with unction or Spirit-empowered boldness, this is the book to read.

Chapell, Bryan. *Christ-Centered Preaching.* Grand Rapids: Baker, 1994.
Chapell is the president of Covenant Theological Seminary in St. Louis, and this is one of the best books available on expository preaching overall.

*Gordon, T. David. *Why Johnny Can't Preach: The Media Have Shaped the Messengers.* Phillipsburg, NJ: P&R Publishing, 2009.
Gordon dissects the problems with much of contemporary preaching and offers suggestions for how sermons can improve. If you wish to be better equipped to evaluate sermons, read this book and pay careful attention to the particular section about how sermons should be evaluated (pages 22–28).

Merida, Tony. *Faithful Preaching.* Nashville: B&H Publishing Company, 2009.
Merida's recently published book is another excellent broad resource on biblical preaching.

*Mohler, R. Albert. *He Is Not Silent: Preaching in a Postmodern World*. Chicago: Moody, 2008.
Mohler explains why "the audacious claim of Christian preaching is that the faithful declaration of the Word of God, spoken through the preacher's voice, is even

more powerful than anything music or image can deliver" (page 17). This is a stirring call for biblical preaching that needs to be heard.

*Ramey, Ken. *Expository Listening: A Handbook for Hearing and Doing God's Word*. The Woodlands, Texas: Kress Biblical Resources, 2010.

Ramey has written an excellent book that encourages God's people about how to listen to the proclaimed Word.

Robinson, Haddon. *Biblical Preaching.* 2nd ed. Grand Rapids: Baker, 2001.

Robinson is arguably the foremost authority on biblical preaching in the English-speaking world. If you want to understand how to prepare an expository sermon, then begin with this book. If the pastoral candidate attended an evangelical seminary, then the chances are good that he will be familiar with this book.